Unveiling
The Great Mystery
of the First Century Church

Volume 1

---- Studies in Biblical Accuracy ----

Mark Atkinson

First Edition 2007

First published 2007

by Lulu Publishers

http://www.lulu.com

ISBN 978-1-84799-925-2

Copyright © Mark Atkinson

All rights reserved.

No part of this publication may be reproduced, stored in a
retrieval system, or transmitted in any form, or by any means,
electrical, mechanical, photocopying, recording or otherwise
without the prior written permission of the author or a licence
permitting restricted copying

Printed and bound by Lulu

Cover Design by 4D Creatives

http://www.4dcreatives.biz

The scriptures used in this book are taken from the Authorised
Version (King James Version).

Further copies of this book may be ordered from:

http://www.thegreatsecret.org

This book is dedicated to

Nathan, Aaron, and Elias.

May you all grow up into Christ in all things and have the joy and peace that comes with believing our God's wonderful, matchless Word.

iv

Table of Contents

Forward	ix
Preface	xi
Part I - The Great Secret in Christ	**1**
Chapter 1: There is a secret	2
Chapter 2: The Greek word "*musterion*"	5
Chapter 3: The Great Secret and the other secrets in the Bible	7
Chapter 4: We speak the Great Secret among the perfect	11
Chapter 5: What is the Great Secret?	14
Chapter 6: More about the Great Secret of the Christ in you	17
Part II - The Revelation of the Great Secret	**21**
Chapter 7: The Great Secret hid in God	22
Chapter 8: The Great Secret was first revealed to the Apostle Paul	24
Chapter 9: If the Devil had known the Great Secret	27
Part III - The Great Secret and the Church Today	**29**
Chapter 10: The Great Secret for Christians today	30
Chapter 11: Leading the Church today	35
Part IV - Comprehending the Great Secret	**39**
Chapter 12: Comprehending the breadth, length, depth and height of the Great Secret	40
Chapter 13: The Great Secret made known by spirit	45
Chapter 14: How to know God and the Great Secret	50
Part V - Foundational Steps in the Great Secret	**53**
Chapter 15: The giver and the gift	54
Chapter 16: Receiving the gift of holy spirit	57
Chapter 17: Born from above	62

Chapter 18: Born again as the sons of God 66

Chapter 19: More about the Great Secret of the Christ in you 68

Chapter 20: Walking in the spirit 72

Chapter 21: The preaching of the Cross and the Great Secret (Part One) 77

Part VI - The Great Secret of Growing Up Into Christ 83

Chapter 22: The heart of the Great Secret 84

Chapter 23: The image of God and the image of the Devil 86

Chapter 24: The mind of Christ and the Great Secret 90

Chapter 25: The Great Secret of growing up into Christ – the image of God 96

Chapter 26: Renewed in "*epignosis*" according to the image of God 101

Part VII - The Great Secret of the One Body of Christ 107

Chapter 27: The truths of the One Body of Christ 108

Chapter 28: The significance of the One Body of Christ 112

Chapter 29: The temple of God and the tabernacle of God 117

Chapter 30: "*Ekklesia*" - called out to the Great Secret in Christ 120

Chapter 31: The Great Secret of the One New Man (Part One) 124

Chapter 32: The Great Secret of the One New Man (Part Two) 130

Chapter 33: The preaching of the Cross and the Great Secret (Part Two) 136

Chapter 34: In the Great Secret not all have the same office 140

Part VIII - The Gospel of the Glory of Our Lord Jesus Christ 153

Chapter 35: The gospel of the glory of Our Lord Jesus Christ 154

Chapter 36: The riches of the glory of the Great Secret (present) 159

Chapter 37: The future of the Great Secret (The hope of glory) 166

Part IX - The Great Secret and the Heart of Man   **173**
Chapter 38: The Great Secret and the heart of man   174

Chapter 39: What the Great Secret looks like on the outside   181

Chapter 40: Let us go on unto perfection   184

Chapter 41: Walking in the Great Secret   193

Part X - The Great Secret and the Purpose of the Ages   **201**
Chapter 42: The administrations of God's households and the
history of the Great Secret   202

Part XI - The Walk of Power   **211**
Chapter 43: The walk of power in the Great Secret   212

Part XII – The Ministers of the Great Secret   **217**
Chapter 44: Apostles, prophets, pastors and teachers of the Great
Secret   218

Chapter 45: Speaking the Great Secret boldly   224

Chapter 46: Understanding the Epistles through the Great Secret   227

Part XIII - The Adversary and the Great Secret   **229**
Chapter 47: The turning away from the Great Secret   230

Chapter 48: The end of the Adversary in the Great Secret   237

Chapter 49: The Adversary's work against the Great Secret   241

Chapter 50: The bright and morning star   247

Chapter 51: The Word of God written in the stars   251

Part XIV - Guarding the Great Secret   **257**
Chapter 52: Guarding the Great Secret and receiving the crown of
righteousness   258

Chapter 53: Guarding the Great Secret and the unity of the spirit   260

Chapter 54: Guarding the Great Secret by holding the head   263

Part XV - The Love of God and the Great Secret   **269**
Chapter 55: The Great Secret in the love of God   270

vii

Part XVI – Conclusion   **275**

Chapter 56: Summary   276

Acknowledgements   279

Epilogue   281

Further Information   283

Forward

by Ian Valentine

Very few people today appreciate the true nature of Christianity. Over the years Christianity has become institutionalised and has fallen into legalism and tradition. It has joined the world's religions as just another religion. Yet at the heart of true Christianity there is a different picture. True Christianity is unique. The apostles and prophets in the first century Christian Church were guardians of a secret knowledge. They taught it to the faithful followers of Jesus Christ. However, for the most part today, this secret knowledge has been lost. This secret teaching of the early Christians is the most powerful knowledge in the entire world. The Bible speaks of its glorious riches and how God wants to make them known. This secret knowledge is at the true heart of Christianity.

I believe that God wants to bring the whole Church today into the unity of the knowledge of this secret teaching. Many Christians are thirsting for the power of God. Many are striving for great outreach. Some are holding fast to the traditions of their elders. Some are seeking a deeper understanding of the Scriptures. However to bind the church together today, Christians must discover their true identity in Christ as revealed in the secret teachings of the first century Church.

I have been a Christian for 28 years and have spent most of this time in small fellowships of likeminded believers who meet in the home. I have taught many, studied intensively, ministered, healed, helped, prayed, and above all loved. I have seen miracles and signs and know first-hand how easily and lovingly God can change the lives of those who accept for themselves this secret knowledge at the heart of true Christianity.

For the last five years I have had the joy to share fellowship with Mark Atkinson. To me, Mark represents the purity of being a true Christian; one born again of God's spirit motivated only by love and serving Him. God has blessed Mark with a sound understanding of "The Great Mystery" concerning Christ and the Church, and has inspired him to write it down for the benefit of the whole Church.

I am overjoyed to be able to write this Forward. I pray that this book can open the scriptures for all Christians today, and that through understanding "The Great Mystery", they will rediscover the glorious truth that powered the early Church. I pray that our loving heavenly Father will work mightily in every reader of this work; that He will wash away every divisive thing that holds back the Church from receiving God's best. I pray that Christians all over the world will discover this secret knowledge so that once again they can move with love and respect for one another, in harmony, doing the will of God with His love, power and strength.

July 2007

Preface

Nearly two thousand years ago, the Lord Jesus Christ appeared to a man named Saul as he was making his way to the city of Damascus in Syria. Just prior to this, Saul had been persecuting the church. He had been consenting to the slaughter of many Christians. Yet, this man Saul was to become one of the greatest Christian apostles of all time. After his conversion, Saul became more widely known by his Greek name Paul. Today, we know him as the Apostle Paul.

Jesus Christ declared that Paul was "a chosen vessel" unto him. Making his way to Damascus, little did Paul realise that God had chosen him to receive the greatest revelation of all time. He was to receive what is Biblically called the Great Mystery or the Great Secret in Christ. This was a secret "which from the beginning of the world had been hid in God". It had been hid from all previous ages and generations and it would be revealed to Paul for the very first time in the history of man. God commissioned Paul to write it down and make it known.

Today, the Great Mystery vitally concerns all those who have been called out in Jesus Christ. It is to be found written in the Bible. Yet, over the centuries many churches have lost this Great Mystery. The true knowledge was replaced with man made errors and wrong teaching. This led to a lack of proper understanding of the Great Mystery but God declares in His Word that He wants to make it known to all His people. This Great Mystery is so vitally important to every Christian that God declares it is a requirement before the Church can become obedient to His will. Today, it is again being made known and it is being spoken of among the faithful in Christ. This book rediscovers what has been lost.

xi

God wants to make it known to every Christian. The Great Mystery concerning Christ and the Church does not have to be a closed book to anyone who hungers and thirsts to know it. God wants His children once again to walk in the greatness of His Son Christ Jesus just like the Apostle Paul and so many others did nearly two thousand years ago. The Great Mystery is our gateway to the real Christian walk. It shows us the power and the love and the glory that is ours in Christ. God wants us all to be fully instructed.

We are about to explore what the Bible really teaches about this Great Mystery and "what are the riches of the glory of this mystery".

Part I - The Great Secret in Christ

Chapter 1: There is a secret

Prayer

Firstly, we should thank our heavenly Father for His great grace. He desires to bring us into the realities of the Great Mystery, or more accurately, the Great Secret that is in Christ.

We also thank Him for all those who have faithfully stood since it was first revealed almost two thousand years ago; for all those who have stood to allow this Great Secret in Christ to be made known. Father....thank you.....and may we and many others rise up to learn these ways and continue in them until the return of Your Son, our Lord Jesus Christ, when he will gather us all unto you. Amen.

Let us begin.

There is a secret

There is a mystery or rather a secret in Christianity that very few people know about. Despite man's ignorance, in God's eyes it is the most important thing for our time, for this Age of Grace that we live in. The purpose of this book is to open up this secret from the Scriptures so that we may all be instructed and come to know and fully comprehend its great truths. It is God's strong desire that all of His sons come into the knowledge of the greatness of this mystery.

Firstly, we need to establish that there is even such a thing as the Mystery.

Paul wrote to the Corinthians challenging them with this statement:

"Howbeit we speak wisdom among them that are perfect......
we speak the wisdom of God in a mystery....."
(1 Corinthians 2:6-7)

Paul also wrote to the Christians in Rome about the Mystery:

"Now to him that of power to stablish you according to my
gospel and the preaching of Jesus Christ according to the
revelation of the mystery, which was kept secret since the
world began" (Romans 16:25)

After that, Paul wrote to the Christians in Ephesus telling them
that God had showed him the Mystery:

"How that by revelation he made known unto me the mystery
(as I wrote afore in few words)" (Ephesians 3:3)

He would then go on to speak about the special mission that God
had set for him:

"And to make all men see what is the fellowship of the
mystery which from the beginning of the world hath been hid
in God...." (Ephesians 3:9)

Paul wrote to the Colossians also telling them about the Mystery:

"Even the mystery which hath been hid from ages and from
generations, but now is made manifest to his saints"
(Colossians 1:26)

These are some of the verses in the Bible that speak of the
Mystery. Clearly, there is a Mystery or Secret in Christianity. So,
what is this Mystery? What does God say about it? What does it
mean? What is its special significance for us? These are some of
the questions that we will shortly be answering. The answers to
these questions can be found by searching out the Bible.

In this book, I will set out for you the beautiful revelation of the
Great Mystery as it is recorded in the Bible. I believe that God

will work with your heart unfolding its real meaning to you and you will then become fully instructed and know what has become the lost Secret of Christianity.

Chapter 2: The Greek word *"musterion"*

"Musterion"

We need to take a look at the word "mystery" in the Bible. The Greek word for mystery is *"musterion"*. Interestingly, this same word was used in many secular writings during the time when the New Testament was written. The word *"musterion"* means the secret of friends or the secret of the king. In a worldly sense, *"musterion"* would refer to the secret knowledge that was revealed to the initiated ones of a fraternity or secret society. Only those members who were in the inner circle would hold the secret knowledge of that fraternity. These secrets would only ever be revealed to the initiated ones who had been allowed to enter within that inner circle. The same is true for Christians and the Christian faith.

The Bible speaks of a secret Biblical teaching. It is a knowledge that is made known among the inner circle of faithful believers. It is possible today for all those who have been called out to Jesus Christ to be initiated into this secret knowledge in Christ.

The Greek *"musterion"* is a derivative of two words, namely: *"mueo"* which means to bring to the place where secrets are made known or literally to initiate into the secrets; and *"mustes"* which refers to the person being brought through the initiation process into the knowledge of the secrets. This understanding becomes very interesting when we look at the Great Mystery in Christ.

More accurately translated "secret"

In the Bible, the word *"musterion"* is translated mystery. However, it is better translated secret or sacred secret. The reason for this is that it is not something that is so mysterious that it cannot be understood but rather it is a secret that God wants to reveal to the spiritually minded Christian, to those who are within the inner circle of faithfulness, to those who are spiritually minded. In other words, it is something that can be taught and known.

In this book, I will use the word 'secret' as it is a more accurate translation of *"musterion"*. I will also refer to the secret concerning Christ and the Church as "the Great Secret" as explained in the next chapter.

Chapter 3: The Great Secret and the other secrets in the Bible

A difference

To have accurate knowledge and understanding, it is important for us to establish that there is a difference between the Great Secret in Christ and the many other secrets or mysteries that are in the Bible. Paul wrote to the Corinthians telling them that he and his fellow labourers were stewards of the mysteries (plural) of God. In other words, there is more than one secret, however, there is only one secret which God calls the Great Secret.

> "Let a man so account of us as of the ministers of Christ, and stewards of the mysteries of God." (1 Corinthians 4:1)

There are many mysteries or secrets in the Bible such as the secrets of the kingdom, the secret of the duration of Israel's blindness, the secret that not all will die, the secret of lawlessness and so on.

The many other secrets

Here are some of them.

There are the secrets of the kingdom which Jesus spoke of:

> "He answered and said unto them, Because it is given unto you to know the mysteries [*musterion = secrets*] of the kingdom of heaven, but to them it is not given"
> (Matthew 13:11)

There is another secret in the Bible that not all will die before Christ returns:

"Behold I shew you a mystery [*musterion = secret*]; we shall not all sleep but we shall all be changed,

In a moment, in the twinkling of an eye, at the last trump: for the trumpet shall sound, and the dead shall be raised incorruptible, and we shall be changed.

For this corruptible must put on incorruption, and this mortal *must* put on immortality

So when this corruptible shall have put on incorruption, and this mortal shall have put on immortality, then shall be brought to pass the saying that is written, Death is swallowed up in victory.

O death, where is thy sting? O grave, where is thy victory?" (1 Corinthians 15:51–55).

There is also the secret regarding the duration of Israel's present blindness and future salvation:

"For I would not, brethren, that you should be ignorant of this mystery [*musterion = secret*], lest ye should be wise in your own conceits; that blindness in part is happened to Israel, until the fulness of the Gentiles be come in.

And so all Israel shall be saved" (Romans 11:25-26)

There is another secret regarding the iniquity of the Adversary:

"For the mystery [*musterion = secret*] of iniquity doth already work: only he who now letteth *will let*, until he be taken out of the way" (2 Thessalonians 2:7)

There is also the secret of understanding the significance of Babylon the Great:

"And upon her forehead was a name written, MYSTERY [*musterion = secret*], BABYLON THE GREAT, THE MOTHER OF HARLOTS AND ABOMINATIONS OF THE EARTH." (Revelation 17:5)

All of the above secrets are only known by those people who have been initiated into them. Otherwise a person would not know their true meaning. They are secrets belonging to the initiated ones.

The Great Secret

However, Ephesians speaks of another mystery which is called the Great Mystery. This mystery or secret is far different from all the others:

"For this cause shall a man leave his father and mother, and shall be joined unto his wife, and they shall be one flesh.

This is a [*the texts read "the"*] great mystery [*musterion = secret*]: but I speak concerning Christ and the church." (Ephesians 5:31-32)

The critical Greek texts read "This is **the** Great Mystery" not simply a mystery. God puts the emphasis by saying that this is the Great Mystery. An even more accurate translation would be 'This is the Great Secret'. The Great Secret refers to Christ and the Church.

As you can see, there are many mysteries or secrets in the Bible. However, to understand the Great Secret, we need to make this distinction between the various other secrets and what God specifically calls "the Great Secret" concerning Christ and the Church. The subject matter of this book is the Great Secret and not the other secrets which are separate subjects in their own right.

This secret stands out above all other secrets in the Bible. God says it is "Great". I believe that you will come to appreciate the greatness and vastness of this secret as you read this book. You will see why God marks out this secret which is above all others in greatness.

Chapter 4: We speak the Great Secret among the perfect

The immature Christians at Corinth

In 1 Corinthians 2:1-2, Paul declared that when he first came to the Corinthians, he came not declaring the Great Secret (in most critical Greek texts the word testimony is this word "*musterion*" meaning the mystery or secret).

> "And I, brethren, when I came to you, came not with excellency of speech or of wisdom, declaring unto you the testimony [*mystery*] of God.
>
> For I determined not to know anything among you, save Jesus Christ and him crucified." (1 Corinthians 2:1-2)

Instead of teaching the Corinthians about the Great Secret, he could only declare the crucifixion of Christ. However, he then goes on to say:

> "Howbeit we speak wisdom among them that are perfect, yet not the wisdom of this world, nor of the princes of this world, that come to nought:
>
> But we speak the wisdom of God in a mystery [*musterion* = secret*], even the hidden *wisdom*, which God ordained before the world unto our glory" (1 Corinthians 2:6-7).

The apostle Paul was challenging the believers in Corinth who were not yet spiritually minded. He was posing a statement to them, "howbeit we speak the wisdom of the Great Secret among the spiritually mature Christians." The Christians at Corinth had shown themselves to be carnally minded through their behaviour.

They were people who did not walk according to God's Word; neither did they know it nor did they understand it. The fundamental truths in Christ had not yet been established in their hearts. Yet Paul was now pointing out to them that the Great Secret was being spoken among the perfect (the spiritually mature or rather the spiritually minded). The carnally minded believers at Corinth had no idea that such a Great Secret even existed. They were not yet ready to be taught the greatness of it. However, he wanted to make them think on these things so he declared that there was something greater available to them when they were ready. Indeed, one day they would be taught the meat of the Great Secret but for the moment, they needed to be nurtured on the milk of the Word first:

> "And I brethren could not speak unto you as unto spiritual but as unto carnal, *even* as unto babes in Christ.
>
> I have fed you with milk and not with meat for hitherto you were not able to *bear it*, neither yet now are ye able" (1 Corinthians 3:1-2)

Shortly, we will look into the meat of this Great Secret in Christ. However, like the Corinthians, not every person in the Christian church today is ready to receive the knowledge of the Great Secret. Some are too young, spiritually speaking, and will need to be fed with the basic principles of the doctrine of Christ first, so that they may grow to be able to receive it. Others will lack the humble heart that is necessary to receive Father's Word and instead will magnify their own thoughts above the Word of God. Others will sadly insist on holding wrong doctrines in their hearts which make the Word of God of none effect to them. However, there are many Christians to whom the wisdom of God can be opened up, so that once again the Great Secret can be spoken of "among the perfect".

For those who are ready

This book has been written for those who desire and are ready to receive the greatness of the secret knowledge in Christ. This book is not for the academic theologian, neither the unfaithful, neither the carnally minded. It takes humility and meekness before God and His Word to begin to understand the wonderful realities of this Great Secret concerning Christ and the Church. We have to let God in His higher wisdom speak to us through His written Word, and this He will do if we are humble before Him to receive His Word.

Then, once known, it will no longer be a secret hidden from you. Rather, you will discover and regain the lost secret of Christianity. However, it does belong to the inner circle of faithful Christians and it is the greatest secret in the world today.

God has called you to be an initiated one in Christ. Father has opened the door and is calling you to enter into that place where the Great Secret in Christ is illuminated in your heart. I know that if you are humble before Him, He will enlighten your heart with these great truths.

Chapter 5: What is the Great Secret?

Two precepts

So, what is the Great Secret? The Great Secret concerning Christ and the church will be unfolded in the rest of this book. However, to begin with, there are two basic precepts in understanding the Great Secret.

Christ in you

Firstly, God declares that the secret is Christ actually in you (in your mortal body):

> "To whom God would make known what are the riches of the glory of this mystery among the Gentiles, which is Christ in you the hope of glory" (Colossians 1:27)

This is one of the major differences that separate out true Christianity from all the religions of the world. The Bible tells us that Christ is in us by way of the gift of holy spirit, which is the spirit of Christ. God has given this spirit to all of us who have confessed that Jesus is Lord and believed that God raised him from the dead. There is a lot for us to learn from the Bible about this spirit of Christ in us and how God wants to see this gift work in us. But for now, just take a moment to think what a privilege it is to have the spirit of Christ dwell in you.

> "....Christ in you, the hope of glory" (Colossians 1:27)

God explains that the secret is Christ in you. Yes, right there in you, in your mortal body. Do you believe God when He says that He has put Christ in you? Do you believe that Christ is actually in you right now as you are reading this book? God declares it to be. God is not a man that He should lie. He has placed Christ in you.

The spirit of Christ is in you right now, in your very being. In this book, we are going to explore what this really means.

The One Body of Christ

The second precept is that people are being called out from both the Jews and the Gentiles to become the One Body of Christ:

> "How that by revelation he made known unto to me the mystery....
>
> That the Gentiles should be fellow heirs and of the same body and partakers of His promise in Christ by the gospel" (Ephesians 3:3-6)

In Old Testament times, it was never conceived that the Gentiles would have equal standing with the Jews. The truth of the One Body of Christ had not been revealed in the Old Testament. This equal standing was revolutionary in the Apostles' day. It was always known that the Gentiles would be blessed with Israel. It was not known, however, that a period of time would come when the Gentiles would be of the same body, and that of Christ himself.

But what is the real significance of the truth of the One Body? The significance of this One Body will be more fully explained in later chapters.

The beginning of understanding the Great Secret

These two precepts are only the beginning of understanding the Great Secret. Our quest is to explore the depths of this secret. The Bible calls these depths "the riches of the glory of this mystery *(musterion = secret)*" (Colossians 1:27). It is God's heart and desire for His children to come to know what these riches of glory are. But for the moment, before we can learn these riches, we need to pass through these two doors of understanding: firstly, to know that it is "Christ in you"; and secondly, that we are the One Body of Christ. These two precepts are the first two steps in comprehending the Great Secret in Christ. Then, we can go forward to understand the multifaceted wisdom of God in the Great Secret. This wisdom will take us far beyond the initial realisation that it is "Christ in you" and that we belong to the One Body.

Chapter 6: More about the Great Secret of the Christ in you

Colossians 1:27

The Epistle to the Colossians is of major significance to our understanding of the Great Secret because here Paul explains that the secret is "Christ in you, the hope of glory".

> "To whom God would make known what are the riches of the glory of this mystery among the Gentiles, which is Christ in you the hope of glory" (Colossians 1:27)

In this verse, the word "in" is a translation of the Greek word "*en*". It is an accurate translation. It is Christ in you, the hope of glory. However, there is more to understand regarding this.

The three aspects of "en" ("Christ in you")

In the context of the Great Secret, the usage of the word "*en*" refers to something that continues to remain within. There are three aspects to this remaining within that we need to learn.

Place

Firstly, this remaining within has regard to place. Christ is in you by his spirit dwelling in your mortal body. The place is your mortal body. So it is written that we have this treasure in earthen vessels:

> "But we have this treasure in earthen vessels, that the excellency of the power may be of God and not of us"
> (2 Corinthians 4:7)

The earthen vessel is your physical body. This is the place.

Time

Secondly, this remaining within has regard to time. The spirit of Christ is in you and continues to remain in you because God does not take it back. It is a gift from God because you need it, and not because you deserve it. In Romans, we learn

"For the gifts and calling of God *are* without repentance." (Romans 11:29)

"Without repentance" means that God does not change His mind after He has declared something as a gift. Therefore, the spirit of Christ is now your spirit forever by God's grace. It is a gift from God to you. The time aspect therefore is that Christ is in you forever throughout all eternity. This is the time element.

Effects

Thirdly, this remaining within also causes effects or has influence on the outside. The remaining of Christ in you can have great effects in the external in terms of the power of God and the nature of God manifest in your life. This is the effects aspect.

These three dimensions of the Christ in you are pivotal to your growth in the Great Secret. Christ, by way of the gift of holy spirit, remains within you. It is this power that you learn to manifest outwardly in your walk and it is the very nature of Christ that you are changed into. We shall look more into these great truths in later chapters.

Is it Christ among you or Christ in you all individually?

Some schools of thought and indeed some translations have rendered the "Christ in you" as being "Christ among you". However, a careful examination reveals that in today's vernacular, "Christ among you" is an error of translation. Such a translation does not capture the finite accuracy of the texts, neither does it convey the three dimensional understanding of the Greek word "*en*" in this context.

The word "you" in Colossians 1:27 is plural because Paul is addressing all believers. Whenever "*en*" is used with a plural noun it is often usual to translate it by the word "among". This is the reason why some translations render this verse as "Christ among you", but the essential meaning is that it is Christ in you all individually. Colossians 1:27 conveys a greater presence than merely Christ among us or in the midst of us or near us. Christ is among us because he is in us all individually. Therefore, "Christ in you" is a more accurate translation.

You should now be convinced that it is not merely Christ with you, upon you, near you or in the midst of you. It is absolutely "Christ in you". Paul said it is Christ in you all individually.

The gift of holy spirit (the spirit of Christ)

The Christ in you refers to the spirit of Christ (holy spirit) that was given at Pentecost. God gave this spirit as a gift. We should understand that a gift is not a wage or a loan. In the Age of Grace in which we now live, the gift of holy spirit is to you as a believer because you have made Jesus Christ your Lord and have believed that God raised him from the dead (Romans 10:9-10 and Acts 2:38). In the rest of this book, you will come to see that the receiving of this spirit is actually God creating Christ in you. This is a sonship spirit which explains how we became the sons of God.

Part II - The Revelation of the Great Secret

Chapter 7: The Great Secret hid in God

God kept the secret hidden from all other ages – It was hid in God

The Great Secret had been hid in God until it was first revealed to the Apostle Paul. It cannot be found in the Old Testament. It was not revealed in the period of Jesus Christ's presence on earth which is recorded in the four gospels. In the Scriptures below, we shall see that God makes a specific distinction between the time that was "then" (which is the period when the Great Secret was hid from all eyes) and the time that is "now" (which is the period of time after Pentecost when the Great Secret was to be finally revealed).

Simply, the Great Secret was hid in God from the beginning of the world.

> "And to make all *men* see what is the fellowship of the mystery, which from the beginning of the world hath been hid in God…….." (Ephesians 3:9a)

Paul's mission was to enlighten the entire Church about the Great Secret that God had previously kept hid in Himself. When something is hid in God, it is past finding out until God decides that it should be revealed. Romans 16:25 tells us that the mystery "was kept secret since the world began, but <u>now</u> is made manifest" to the saints.

> "Now to Him that is of power to stablish you according to my gospel and the preaching of Jesus Christ, according to the revelation of the mystery, which was kept secret since the world began

But now is made manifest and by the scriptures of the prophets, according to the commandment of the everlasting God made known to all nations for the obedience of faith." (Romans 16:25-26)

Similarly, Colossians tells us that the secret was hid from all ages and generations until the now:

"*Even* the mystery which hath been hid from ages and generations, but <u>now</u> is made manifest to His saints" (Colossians 1:26)

The Great Secret had been hid from all ages and generations. Likewise, Ephesians 3:5 tells us that in other ages, it

"…was not made known unto the sons of men as it is <u>now</u> revealed unto His holy apostles and prophets by the Spirit".

The Epistles

During the Old Testament times the Great Secret was hid in God, therefore it cannot be found in the Old Testament scriptures. God has deemed that it is revealed only in the Epistles. This revelation may put the Epistles in a new light for you.

It helps to understand that the riches of what Jesus Christ accomplished for us are revealed only in the Epistles. Therefore, we ought to earnestly seek out the Epistles to see what riches God wants to reveal to us.

Chapter 8: The Great Secret was first revealed to the Apostle Paul

"My gospel"

God first revealed the Great Secret to the Apostle Paul. In Romans 16:25, Paul refers to the Great Secret as "my gospel". In Ephesians Paul tells us that God had given to him the dispensation of the grace of God for all believers in this age. The word "dispensation" here means government administration. God gave to Paul the full instructions as to how He wanted His affairs in the Church to be administered in this Age of Grace that we now live in.

"If ye have heard of the dispensation of God which is given me to you-ward

How that by revelation He made known unto me the mystery" (Ephesians 3:1-3)

God made known to Paul the Great Secret by revelation.

"Now to Him that is of power to stablish you according to my gospel and the preaching of Jesus Christ, according to the revelation of the mystery, which was kept secret since the world began

But now is made manifest and by the scriptures of the prophets, according to the commandment of the everlasting God made known to all nations for the obedience of faith." (Romans 16:25-26)

The Word says that God is able to establish you and I in the greatness of Paul's gospel which is the Great Secret concerning Christ and the Church.

The gospel according to Paul

The gospel of Jesus Christ that Paul preached was different than the four gospels of Matthew, Mark, Luke and John. Paul's gospel goes much further and deeper into the riches of Christ. His preaching was according to the revelation of the Great Secret that he had received. This gospel had been kept secret, hid in God, until He revealed it to the Apostle Paul.

The four Gospels document the prophecies, life, death, and resurrection of our Lord Jesus Christ. He came as Israel's King, but they rejected and killed him. However, the Epistles of Paul document the riches that God has accomplished for us through the work of Jesus Christ. These riches could not be made known until after the death, resurrection and ascension of our Lord Jesus Christ and after the giving of holy spirit on Pentecost.

"Scriptures of the Prophets" (The Epistles are the writings of truth)

The following verse refers to the Great Secret. Here, Paul explains that the Great Secret is recorded in the Epistles.

> "But now is made manifest and by the scriptures of the prophets, according to the commandment of the everlasting God, made known to all nations for the obedience of faith." (Romans 16:26)

The above verse in Romans is full of richness but first we need to sharpen the translation so that its real meaning can be opened up to us. The phrase "the scriptures of the prophets" does not mean the scriptures in the Old Testament. This is because the Old Testament scriptures cannot make known the Great Secret since we now know that God has said that He had kept it hid in Himself from all ages until it was revealed to Paul. The Great Secret was never revealed to Isaiah, Jeremiah, Daniel and others because it was hid in God and past finding out. No prophet in the

Old Testament times knew it. Therefore, the phrase "the scriptures of the prophets" in Romans simply cannot refer to the Old Testament prophets. Rather, these words literally mean "the prophetic writings" or more accurately "the writings of truth". This phrase specifically refers to the Epistles written by Paul, to whom God had made known the Great Secret by revelation.

He had given Paul the administration of the Grace of God. He had revealed the Great Secret to Paul and commanded him to write it down in the Epistles and thereby make it known to all nations. This is the accuracy of verse 26. The Great Secret is progressively unfolded in the writings of Paul which are also known as the Church Epistles (Romans, Corinthians, Galatians, Ephesians, Philippians, Colossians, and Thessalonians) and the Pastoral Epistles (Timothy, Titus and Philemon), and the Epistle to the Hebrews. These are the prophetic writings or the writings of truth.

So let's read verse 26 again:

> "But now [*the Great Secret*] is made manifest [*revealed by spirit*] and by the scriptures of the prophets [*the Epistles of Paul, which are the writings of truth*], according to the commandment of the everlasting God, [*is*] made known to all nations for the obedience of faith." (Romans 16:26)

God commanded Paul to write it down so that the Great Secret could be preserved even for us today. It has been said that many churches have lost the true knowledge of Christianity; nevertheless you and I have the heritage of the Great Secret preserved in the Epistles, the writings of truth and that by God's commandment to Paul. He fulfilled God's commandment by writing it down.

Chapter 9: If the Devil had known the Great Secret

The Devil is now faced with more than one Jesus Christ

We now know that Christ is in every believer. This is the beginning of understanding the Great Secret. However, the startling truth is that this secret is so great that if the Devil had known it he would not have crucified Jesus Christ.

> "Which none of the princes of this world knew: for had they known it, they would not have crucified the Lord of glory." (1 Corinthians 2:8)

In John 14:30, Jesus Christ called the Adversary, who is the Devil, "the prince of this world". Paul wrote in Ephesians 2:2 calling the Devil "the prince of the power of the air". The word "princes" in 1 Corinthians 2:8 refers to the Devil and his ruling devil spirits. So great is this secret of Christ and the Church that if the devils had known it beforehand, they would not have crucified Jesus Christ. Why? The answer is because ever since Pentecost, the Devil and his kingdom are no longer faced with just one Jesus Christ, but rather they are now faced with millions of believers who have "Christ in them". By crucifying Jesus Christ, the Adversary the Devil had now attracted to himself an insurmountable problem. In the spirit realm, he is now faced with millions of Christ spirits. That's why today, one of the Adversary's top priorities is to hinder the knowledge of this Great Secret of the Christ in you. However, he is destined to fail in this feat against God.

Greater is the Christ in you than the Devil in the world

The Devil crucified Jesus Christ, but when he was raised to life again by the Father, he overcame the Devil and made a public spectacle of him and all his devil spirits. Now Christ is far greater and far more powerful than the Devil. The Christ in you is greater than the Devil and all the devil spirits in the world put together; and because it is Christ in you, God declares to the world that you have already overcome them:

> "Ye are of God, little children, and have overcome them: because greater is he that is in you, than he that is in the world." (1 John 4:4)

Greater is the Christ in you than the Devil and his entire host that is in the whole world. Again, it is Christ actually in you; in your mortal body:

> "For whatsoever is born of God overcometh the world: and this is the victory that overcometh the world, *even* our faith.
>
> Who is he that overcometh the world, but he that believeth that Jesus is the Son of God." (1 John 5:4-5)

Whatsoever is born of God has already overcome the world. You have been born of God, born from above because the Almighty Father has put Christ in you. Praise God! How great is the wisdom of God in this secret which He had kept hid in Himself until He revealed it to the Apostle Paul.

Part III - The Great Secret and the Church Today

Chapter 10: The Great Secret for Christians today

What God wants Christians to believe?

We need to ask ourselves the question "do we accurately believe exactly what God wants us to believe, or have we allowed other things to stray in, take root or even gain prominence?"

Within Christendom today, there are many doctrines and ideologies. Not all of these come from God. Some indeed come from man and some from the devils. Sadly, there are many children of God who are being tossed to and fro with doctrines that have not come from God.

This is not God's will at all for His people. Our Heavenly Father is all wise and He has already chosen what He wants us to believe. It would therefore be wise on our part to take His counsel to heart and walk accordingly.

The "obedience to the faith" and the "obedience of faith"

In the Epistle to the Romans, God sets out very plainly what He wants us to believe. There are two particular phrases about faith that stand out: the "obedience **to the** faith" and the "obedience **of** faith". These two phrases are different in context and mean different things but both directly refer to the content of what you believe. The first one is at the beginning of Romans; the second one is at the end of Romans. One deals with the Gospel of God and the other deals with the Gospel of the Great Secret of Christ and the Church.

At the beginning of Romans, we read about the Gospel of God concerning Jesus Christ. This gospel was never kept secret. It was actually revealed in the Old Testament. It was promised and made known beforehand, and it deals with the resurrection of Jesus Christ. God wants man to believe this gospel about His Son Jesus Christ so that man can be saved and thereafter become obedient to "the faith" which is later revealed as the Great Secret.

"Paul, a servant of Jesus Christ, called *to be* an apostle, separated unto the gospel of God,

(Which he had promised afore by his prophets in the holy scriptures,)

Concerning his Son Jesus Christ our Lord, which was made of the seed of David according to the flesh;

And declared *to be* the Son of God with power, according to the spirit of holiness, by the resurrection from the dead:

By whom we have received grace and apostleship, for obedience to the faith among all nations, for his name" (Romans 1:1-5)

In this first part of Romans, God declares that the Gospel of God was for the "obedience to the faith". God wants man to first believe that Jesus Christ is His Son and that He raised him up from the dead to save all mankind. This was never a secret, but the apostles taught man to believe this gospel so that man could be saved. When a person is saved, he can then go on to become obedient to the true faith, which is the Great Secret concerning Christ and the Church. Our Father always had a vision beyond the Gospel of God: He wants us to go on to the Great Secret. The phrase "the faith" means the true faith of Jesus Christ which culminates in the Great Secret. This is what God wants us all to believe.

So, at the end of Romans, we read about a new gospel. Paul didn't call this new gospel "the Gospel of God". But rather, God had commanded Paul to call it "my gospel", that is Paul's gospel. Here, God was marking out Paul because He had given to Paul a gospel that was different from all others. It was the preaching of Jesus Christ according to the revelation of the Great Secret.

This was something far more than the earlier gospel. Unlike the Gospel of God concerning his Son, Paul's gospel had not been promised before. Instead, it had been hidden, kept secret since the world began. It had been hid in God. It could not be found in the Old Testament writings of the prophets. Paul was to receive it for the very first time in the history of man. Moreover, God had now commanded Paul to write it down in the Epistles. And it was now being made known for the "obedience of faith".

This set a new standard for Christians in terms of what we should believe. God's heart is that we should go on to believe this great revelation. It was a new gospel revealed by God to Paul.

> "Now to Him that is of power to stablish you according to my gospel and the preaching of Jesus Christ, according to the revelation of the mystery, which was kept secret since the world began
>
> But now is made manifest and by the scriptures of the prophets, according to the commandment of the everlasting God made known to all nations for the obedience of faith" (Romans 16:25-26)

So God commanded that the secret was to be made known for the "obedience of faith". There is a special obedience to God which is only gained by believing the Great Secret. This is the obedience that is produced only when the Great Secret is believed and practised. This is God's will for all Christians.

His Word is so simple that not even a child should err therein. The phrases "obedience to the faith" and "obedience of faith" directly refer to the content of what you believe. After we have received salvation (the Gospel of God), He now wants us all to move on to believe the Great Secret and not to wander off with other things or in other directions.

He wants us to obey Him by believing the secret. When the content of our believing is the Great Secret, only then have we reached the "obedience of faith". Without believing the Great Secret, it is impossible today to arrive at the "obedience of faith" or rather, the obedience that is found after believing and practising the Great Secret.

Clearly, God's will is for all Christians to progress much further than the Gospel of God. There is a further gospel that deals with all the great riches that Jesus Christ has accomplished for us. God wants to enrich us with these things but, in order for us to have these riches evident in our lives, He requires that we pursue the "obedience of faith". Otherwise, the many blessings of the Great Secret will simply lay dormant within us.

Apostles, prophets, pastors and teachers

I often think to myself how can Christians today obey God in these regards if the Great Secret is not taught? The apostles, prophets, pastors and teachers in the church have the responsibility for making it known among God's people so that everyone's believing can become obedient to God, and so everyone can reach the "obedience of faith" in the presence of our heavenly Father.

Your believing

Have you yet reached the 'obedience of faith'? Do you want your believing to be judged as obedient by God? Simply, it is the believing of the Great Secret which is the test standard as to whether your own believing is obedient or disobedient to God. The "obedience to the faith" and the "obedience of faith" are no small matters with God. We shall come to see later in this book why God wants us to believe the Great Secret and why we should be obedient in these regards.

God's wise counsel can be trusted far more than anything that man can say.

Chapter 11: Leading the Church today

How God wants the Church to be governed

Have you ever asked yourself how would God want the affairs of His household governed? This is a good question to ask in view of the many different and opposing directions that the various groups and churches are moving in. Well, the Bible is clear and specific about this in the same manner as it is regarding the "obedience of faith". Again, it relates directly to the Great Secret.

"Oikonomia"

There is a Greek word, *"oikonomia"*, which Paul uses in his writings that is significant in understanding God's will in this area. *"Oikonomia"* is made up of two words: *"oikos"* meaning house or household and *"nomia"* meaning government or administration. Literally, *"oikonomia"* means household government or household administration and refers to **exactly how God wants the affairs of His household to be administered.** In the Bible, this word is often translated dispensation or fellowship, but really, the accuracy of the original refers to how God wants His household governed. Let's take a look at some of the verses where Father sets this out:

> "Whereof I am made a minister according to the dispensation [*oikonomia = household administration*] of God which is given to me for you to fulfil the word of God
>
> Even the mystery [*musterion = the Great Secret*] which hath been hid from ages and from generations, but now is made manifest to his saints

To whom God would make known what are the riches of the glory of this mystery [*musterion = the Great Secret*] among the Gentiles; which is Christ in you the hope of glory" (Colossians 1: 25-27)

By revelation, God gave to Paul the details of how He wants his household to be administered or governed. Paul states that the correct administration or government of God's household is the mystery *(musterion = the Great Secret)*. This is how God wants his affairs to be administered, even today. Anything else is either wrong or falls short of God's standard.

In Ephesians, Paul explains this further:

> "If ye have heard of the dispensation [*oikonomia = household administration*] of the grace of God which is given me to you-ward
>
> How that by revelation He made known unto me the mystery [*musterion = the Great Secret*] (as I wrote afore in a few words
>
> Whereby, when ye read, ye may understand my knowledge in the mystery [*musterion*] of Christ)
>
> Which in other ages was not made known unto the sons of men as it is now revealed unto His holy apostles and prophets by the Spirit." (Ephesians 3:2-5)

The "rules" of the administration of God's household were given to Paul and these "rules" are defined as the mystery *(musterion = the Great Secret)*. God gave the details of this administration to Paul "to you-ward"; this phrase refers to the whole Church; Paul received from God how He wanted the affairs of the Church to be administered. The leaders (apostles, prophets, pastors and teachers) in the Church today are to ensure that this Great Secret is at the pinnacle of how God's affairs are administered.

This Great Secret should be taught and should be at the heart of the government of the household of God. Many churches and groups have yet to become obedient to God's will in these respects.

"To make all men see"

The leaders in God's household today have a job to do. Paul then goes on to explain this in even greater and more striking detail:

> "And to make all men see what is the fellowship [*oikonomia = household administration*] of the mystery [*musterion = the Great Secret*], which from the beginning of the world has been hid in God…" (Ephesians 3:9)

As a leader in the first century church, Paul's task was to shed light and illuminate the Great Secret so that everyone in the household could be enlightened to firstly understand what the Great Secret is all about and secondly to understand how it is God's will for the affairs of the household to be governed by it.

"…charge some that they teach no other doctrine"

Paul wrote to Timothy instructing him that that he must charge some in the church that they teach the doctrine of the Great Secret and not forge a different direction:

> "As I besought thee to abide still at Ephesus, when I went into Macedonia, that thou mightest charge some that they teach no other doctrine,
>
> Neither give heed to fables and endless genealogies, which minister questions, rather than godly edifying [Gr. "*oikonomia*"] which is in faith: *so do.*" (1 Timothy 1:3-4)

There were some in the church that would not obey God's will regarding the preaching of Jesus Christ according to the revelation of the Great Secret. Rather, they sought to take the emphasis away from the secret and place it on other things. This is often true, even today. However, Paul asked Timothy to stay at Ephesus to charge some of them that they teach no other doctrine but the secret. The words "godly edifying" in verse 4 are this Greek word "*oikonomia*" which refers to the household administration of the secret. Paul was informing Timothy their false teachings would give rise to foolish questions rather than bring people into God's will and blessings in the administration of the secret. Timothy was to charge them that they should come back to the Great Secret and concentrate on teaching it so that they would be in accordance with the will of God.

In summary

God's word is clear. He wants us to believe the Great Secret so that we attain to the "obedience of faith". The gospel of the Great Secret is exactly what He wants us to believe today. And this is how He wants us to grow spiritually too. His standard for the government of His household is also the Great Secret. Leaders in the household today should ensure that the Great Secret is given the supremacy that God gives it. It should be taught and made known so that all members of the household can become illuminated. It should be at the very centre of the teachings in our churches today. Sadly though, at the point of writing it isn't. However, I see that one day it will be at the very heart of our organisations as it once again becomes known. Then, Christians all over the world will once again walk in the greatness of this secret in Christ.

Part IV - Comprehending the Great Secret

Chapter 12: Comprehending the breadth, length, depth and height of the Great Secret

God's heart

In this chapter we are going to look specifically at God's heart and desire in making known the Great Secret in Christ. We shall see that He has commanded for it to be made known to all nations. It is absolutely God's will for you and I to comprehend the secret and also to have all the depths of this knowledge evident in our lives. He wants us to walk in the greatness of Christ.

God wants all mankind to be saved and to come to know (*Gr. "epignosis"*) the Great Secret in Christ

Without a shadow of doubt, God's ultimate will is for all mankind to be saved by His son Jesus Christ and then for all mankind to come into the full mature knowledge of the truth.

> "Who will have all men to be saved and come unto the
> knowledge of the truth" (1 Timothy 2:4)

The word knowledge in this verse is the Greek "*epignosis*". It is the strongest word for knowledge in the Bible and refers to the full mature knowledge of the Great Secret in Christ. It is a knowledge which is gained by experiencing the truth first; then having experienced it, a person would then be positioned upon that knowledge as having been matured by it. In other words, the Great Secret in Christ can only really be known by experiencing it.

This Great Secret in Christ is for living, not merely for head knowledge. We will really come to know the Great Secret as we believe what the Word of God says about it and then we go on to live it in all its fullness.

God commanded that it should be written down

We have seen earlier how that God commanded Paul to write down the Great Secret in the Church Epistles so that it could be made known to all nations.

> "Now to Him that is of power to stablish you according to my gospel and the preaching of Jesus Christ, according to the revelation of the mystery, which was kept secret since the world began
>
> But now is made manifest and by the scriptures of the prophets, according to the commandment of the everlasting God made known to all nations for the obedience of faith." (Romans 16:25-26)

God commanded Paul to write it down in the Scriptures and to make it known to all nations. The word Gentiles here simply means nations. This includes making it known to you and me.

God wants us to see and be enlightened

The ministry of the Apostle Paul was to make everyone in the Church see what is the secret and how the church should move forwards with it.

> "And to make all men see what is the fellowship of the mystery which from the beginning of the world hath been hid in God...." (Ephesians 3:9)

The word fellowship in verse 9 is "*oikonomia*" which as we have seen means household government or administration. God's will is for everyone in the church to see what this really means.

The word 'see' in verse 9 is the Greek word *"photizo"* which means to brighten up, to shed light upon, or to illuminate. God worked with Paul in order to enlighten all members in the Church regarding the details of this Great Secret in Christ. God will illuminate this Great Secret to us also.

God will establish us in the Great Secret

God will absolutely establish you and I in this Great Secret in Christ if we go to Him and humble ourselves before the greatness of His Word.

> "Now to Him that is of power to stablish you according to my gospel and the preaching of Jesus Christ, according to the revelation of the mystery, which was kept secret since the world began" (Romans 16:25)

It is God who will establish us. He will position us in the greatness of the secret. He will enlighten us so that we will have an in depth spiritual perception and awareness of the greatness of the Christ within and the full knowledge and understanding of the secret.

God wants to make known what are the riches of the glory of this secret

In the letter to the Colossians, Paul raises our understanding even further regarding God's heart and the secret.

> "To whom God would make known what are the riches of the glory of this mystery among the Gentiles, which is Christ in you the hope of glory" (Colossians 1:27)

Not only does God want to make known the Great Secret in Christ but He also wants to make known what are the riches of the glory of this secret – this is more. Later, we shall take a look at what these riches are. Clearly, God wants to make them known to us. His joy is to see you and I walk in all of these riches.

God wants you to comprehend the breadth, length, depth and height of the Great Secret

There is an astounding verse in Ephesians which explains that God wants us to comprehend the breadth, length, depth and height of this Great Secret.

> "May be able to comprehend with all saints what *is* the
> breadth, and length, and depth, and height" (Ephesians 3:18)

Many have misunderstood what the Apostle Paul was saying here. This verse does not refer to the love of God because we know that the love of God cannot be constrained by any breadth, length, depth and height. Rather, the love of God is boundless. There simply is no boundary that would ever capture or contain the love of God, except our heavenly Father Himself. However, the Great Secret on the other hand does have boundaries. The Great Secret does have a breadth, a length, a depth and a height. Furthermore, this verse in chapter 3 is in the context of the administration of the Great Secret and this is exactly what Paul was talking about. It is available today to really understand the Great Secret in all its depth. God declares that He wants us to comprehend the shape of it: what it looks like; the entire breadth of it; the entire length of it; the entire depth of it; and the entire height of it. The Greek word for "comprehend" in this verse is "*katalambano*". It means to attain by taking possession. It is akin to "*epignosis*" which means to be matured through the knowledge that comes only by experiencing the subject. These truths are God's will for you and I in relation to the Great Secret. He wants us to attain to the Great Secret; to know it experientially; and in making it our own to thereby possess it.

God wants us to be comforted by the full assurance of understanding the secret

God also wants us all to be comforted and assured by fully understanding the secret.

> "That their hearts might be comforted, being knit together in love, and unto all the riches of the full assurance of understanding, to the acknowledgment of the mystery..." (Colossians 2:2)

The word acknowledgment in verse 2 is this word "*epignosis*" which we have just looked at. It means the full mature knowledge by experiencing it. After knowing the Great Secret in Christ by experience, Father wants us to then go on to be comforted and assured by it. He also wants our minds to be knit together by the full assurance of understanding and by fully knowing the Great Secret. This full assurance of understanding will enrich your life.

How beautiful God's Word truly is. The Great Secret brings great comfort to all of us who really want to know.

Chapter 13: The Great Secret made known by spirit

God makes it known by spirit

Paul explains that the secret was made known to him by revelation.

> "But I certify you, brethren, that the gospel which was preached of me is not after man.
>
> For I neither received it of man neither was I taught it, but by the revelation of Jesus Christ." (Galatians 1:11-12)
>
> "How that by revelation He made known unto me the mystery" (Ephesians 3:3)

God revealed the secret to Paul by the spirit. He showed Paul what the secret was all about. This is a great key in how we too are to receive this knowledge and understanding of the Great Secret. Paul received this revelation by the spirit both for himself and for the rest of the church. He recorded the revelation of the Great Secret in the Epistles.

When reading the Epistles, we must remember that the overarching context is the Great Secret. When we receive the Word of God in the Epistles with this in mind then lots of scriptures fall into place. So Paul prayed that God would reveal the true wisdom of the Great Secret to us also:

> "That the God of our Lord Jesus Christ, the Father of glory, may give unto you the spirit of wisdom and revelation in the knowledge of him" (Ephesians 1:17)

God gives us this revelation because we have the spirit of Christ in us. Today, God will reveal the breadth, length, depth and height of this Great Secret to us by the spirit as we believe what the written Word says about the secret. He will reveal and unfold the meaning of His Word to us. Our God and Father can unfold His true understanding of the Great Secret to us via the spirit in us.

After Paul had received the revelation of the Great Secret, he then spoke that Word to those who could receive it. God also commanded him to write down the secret in what we know today as the Epistles. By revelation, God had first worked with Paul to nurture his growth in the secret. In this, Paul came to know the Great Secret by experientially living the Christ in him according to what God was revealing to him. Afterwards, God would reveal the specific words for each Epistle so that it could be made known to all nations.

Paul had received the entire scope of the Great Secret. The administration of the Great Secret had been given to him, and as we have seen, God commanded him to call it "my gospel", that is Paul's gospel because it had been entrusted to him. However, through Paul's spoken and written ministry, God then raised up other apostles and prophets to whom He could reveal the Great Secret in Christ so that Paul also had fellow workers in the ministry in his day.

> "Which in other ages was not made known unto the sons of men, as it is now revealed unto his holy apostles and prophets by the spirit" (Ephesians 3:5)

"Eye hath not seen, nor ear heard…."

The secret is properly made known to us by God revealing it and then we walk out in that revealed wisdom of God. This occurs when we read the written Word or when we call it to mind from memory. God will also reveal it when the Word is spoken to us for example in a teaching or when we are being ministered to, or from a teaching CD or even reading this book. However, man cannot come to the knowledge and understanding of the secret without God working in him.

> "But as it is written, Eye hath not seen, nor ear heard, neither have entered into the heart of man, the things which God hath prepared for them that love him" (1 Corinthians 2:9)

In other ages, the Great Secret was hid in God. This secret was too great for man's heart to figure out. It never entered into the heart of man. So even today, man's heart alone cannot search out the secret. The Word of God concerning the secret must first be preached to us then the Spirit of God reveals to us the depths of this secret.

> ".... that I should preach among the Gentiles the unsearchable riches of Christ" (Ephesians 3:8b)

The word "unsearchable" here means untraceable. These riches of Christ in you could not be traced in anything that had so far been revealed. They were not revealed in the Old Testament and are quite simply past finding out without God revealing them through the spirit. Today, however, God is revealing them. He has declared that this Age of Grace we live in today is the time for the riches to be revealed. He will reveal the Great Secret to us.

The deep things of God

The deep things of God are the depths of the Great Secret in Christ. These are revealed to us by the spirit.

47

"But God hath revealed *them* unto us by his spirit: for the spirit searcheth all things, yea, the deep things of God". (1 Corinthians 2:10)

Paul then goes on to tell us that we have received the spirit so that we may know the Great Secret.

"Now we have received, not the spirit of the world, but the spirit which is of God; that we might know the things that are freely given to us of God" (1 Corinthians 2:12)

The deep things of God must be spiritually discerned. This literally means that the deep things of the Great Secret can only be truly known through looking at them with the spirit from God. This is because they are spiritually discerned.

"But the natural man receiveth not the things of the Spirit of God; for they are foolishness unto him; neither can he know them, because they are spiritually discerned." (1 Corinthians 2:14)

Only the spirit of God can truly show us the deep things of the Great Secret. When the Word of God is taught to us, it is God who opens up the meaning. Only the spirit of God can lead us into the deep things of God. The natural man is the man who does not have the spirit from God in him. God says that he cannot know these things because they are foolishness to him. Simply, he has no spirit from God to show him.

You and I have the spirit from God. He will faithfully continue to show us the deep things of the secret:

"For God, who commanded the light to shine out of darkness, hath shined in our hearts, to give the light of the knowledge of the glory of God in the face of Jesus Christ.

But we have this treasure in earthen vessels, that the excellency of the power may be of God and not of us." (2 Corinthians 4:6-7)

God will continue to illuminate this Great Secret in our hearts and He will do this until our Lord Jesus Christ returns.

Chapter 14: How to know God and the Great Secret

How to know God

Man cannot truly know God without love. It's impossible. Paul wrote to the Corinthians that knowledge simply inflates a person but love builds up a person in God's eyes.

"Knowledge puffeth up, but charity edifieth.

And if any man think that he knoweth any thing, he knoweth nothing as he ought to know.

But if any man love God, the same is known of him." (1 Corinthians 8:1-3)

Man may think he knows God, but the truth is that he doesn't know anything as he really ought to know. Rather, only those who love God really know Him. It is in the love of God that the true knowledge of Him is acquired. The extent to which you love God is the same extent to which you know Him. In other words, your knowledge of God is measured by or is equal to your love of the Father because God is love. If any man loves God, the same (i.e. God) is known of him. The Apostle John wrote on similar lines:

"Beloved, let us love one another: for love is of God; and every one that loveth is born of God, and knoweth God.

He that loveth not knoweth not God; for God is love." (1 John 4:7-8)

Theologians may know many things about the written Word in the Bible. But if they do not love God, then it is all pointless for they will not know God experientially. Our Father God is the subject of the Bible. Jesus Christ gave his life that we may experientially know his Father.

How to know the Great Secret

God's heart is for us to know the Great Secret. However, the Great Secret cannot be fully comprehended without us being rooted and grounded in the love of God first:

> "That Christ may dwell in your hearts by faith; that ye, being rooted and grounded in love,
>
> May be able to comprehend with all saints what is the breadth, and length, and depth, and height;" (Ephesians 3:17-18)

When Christ dwells in our hearts by believing, and when we are rooted and grounded in the love of God, then we can go on to comprehend the length, breadth, depth and height of the Great Secret. This is an awesome promise in God's Word but being rooted and grounded in the love of God first is a prerequisite before fully knowing the secret. In other words, the secret can only be seen through the eyes of God's love.

The faith of Jesus Christ

Before comprehending the length, breadth, depth and height of the secret, it is also required that Christ dwells in our hearts by believing. This means that our believing grows into the faith of our Lord Jesus Christ. We will then believe what he believes which is the Word of God, and in particular the Great Secret. Christ shall dwell in our hearts and we will see as he sees. However, we also learn that the greatness of the faith of Jesus Christ is worked by love:

51

"For in Jesus Christ neither circumcision availeth anything, nor uncircumcision; but faith which worketh by love." (Galatians 5:6)

The word "worketh" here is the Greek word "*energeo*" which refers to the effects or the power of the faith of Jesus Christ in us. The Great Secret was provided to us in love and it is energized within us by love. It comes to fulfilment in love.

When we live by the faith of Jesus Christ so that Christ dwells in our hearts and when we are also rooted and grounded in the love of God, then we can begin to know God. And we can then go on to truly know the Great Secret in Christ. Without the love of God in our hearts, it is impossible to comprehend the breadth, length, depth and height of the Great Secret in Christ.

(see also Chapter 26: Renewed in "epignosis" according to the image of God)

Part V - Foundational Steps in the Great Secret

Chapter 15: The giver and the gift

The importance of accurate understanding

Today, there is a lot of confusion in the churches about the gift of holy spirit that came at Pentecost and what the gift truly is. Many things are spoken about the gift of holy spirit that are unsound and have no basis in the Scriptures. However, more significantly, such misunderstandings have prevented many Christians from going on to properly understand the Great Secret in Christ.

Before anyone can discern the Great Secret, they must first have an accurate understanding of what God says about the gift of holy spirit. If we allow error and the Devil's lies about this gift to take root in our minds, then we will simply not be able to receive the great revelation of the secret in our minds. Therefore, in the next few chapters I am going to set out for you the accuracy and integrity of God's Word regarding this precious gift of holy spirit that came at Pentecost.

The difference between the giver and the gift

Many Christians have wrongly been taught that there is no difference between God who is Holy and Spirit and the gift of holy spirit that came at Pentecost. Yet, there is an enormous difference between God the Giver who is Holy Spirit and His gift to us which is also holy spirit. If we fail to make this distinction and get these two important differences mixed up, then we will not be able to understand the new birth in Christ. And God's will for us in the riches of the glory of the secret will become blurred.

54

God is both Holy and Spirit

The Bible says that God is both Holy and Spirit. Jesus called God "Holy Father":

> "Holy Father, keep through thine own name those whom thou hast given me, that they may be one as we *are*." (John 17:11)

In the Old Testament, there is a record of the seraphims standing above the throne of God. They described God as "Holy, holy, holy":

> "And one cried unto another, and said, Holy, holy, holy, *is* the Lord of hosts: the whole earth *is* full of his glory." (Isaiah 6:3)

God is Holy. Jesus also taught that God is Spirit:

> "God *is* a Spirit: and they that worship him must worship *him* in spirit and in truth."(John 4:24)

In this verse, Jesus firstly speaks of God who is Spirit and then refers to the gift of holy spirit that the true worshippers would receive so that they could worship Him in spirit and truth. Jesus Christ accurately made the distinction. Therefore, when we read the word of God, we shall be mindful of this distinction as to what is being referred to: whether it is God the Giver or whether it is His gift; both are holy and both are spirit. Let's take a look at couple of records:

> "That which is born of the Spirit is spirit." (John 3:6)

Here, Jesus was speaking to Nicodemus about both God the Giver who is Spirit and the gift which is spirit.

There is another record in Acts which contains reference to both in the same verse:

"And they were all filled with the Holy Ghost, and began to speak with other tongues, as the Spirit gave them utterance." (Acts 2:4)

In this verse, the Apostles were all filled with holy spirit (which is the gift of holy spirit) and then they spoke the words given to them by the Spirit (who is God the Giver).

Knowing this distinction will deepen your understanding of many scriptures. You will be blessed how clear many scriptures become when you appreciate the distinction between the Holy Spirit who is God and the gift of holy spirit which was promised to us and came at Pentecost.

Chapter 16: Receiving the gift of holy spirit

The promise of the Father

The people of Israel knew that Adam had lost the spirit in the very day when he disobeyed God in the garden of Eden. In the Old Testament times, God would put His spirit upon the prophets but it was always conditional upon their faithfulness. When they became unfaithful, God would take back the spirit from them. However, Israel also knew from the words of the prophets that the time would come when the spirit of God would be restored to His people. Jesus knew this and spoke of this very thing as the gift of holy spirit and as "the promise of the Father". Jesus told the Apostles to stay in Jerusalem and to:

> "….wait for the promise of the Father, which, *saith* he, ye have heard of me. For John truly baptised with water; but ye shall be baptized with the Holy Ghost not many days hence." (Acts 1:4-5)

Jesus instructed the Apostles that the promise of the Father is the gift of holy spirit.

The gift of holy spirit shall be in you

A time would come when the spirit from God would dwell in them forever. Rather than just being with them or upon them, the spirit would be inside them.

> "And I will pray the Father, and he shall give you another Comforter, that he may abide with you for ever;
>
> *Even* the spirit of truth…. for he dwelleth with you, and shall be in you" (John 14:17)

There is an enormous difference between the spirit being with or upon a person and the spirit being within a person forever. However, Jesus spoke of these matters before Pentecost.

"when the day of Pentecost was fully come..."

We now know that the gift of holy spirit that Jesus was referring to came on the day of Pentecost. Chapter Two in Acts records the outpouring of the gift of holy spirit.

> "And when the day of Pentecost was fully come, they were all with one accord in one place......
>
> And they were all filled with the Holy Ghost, and began to speak with other tongues, as the Spirit gave them utterance," (Acts 2:1 and 4)

For the very first time in history, man had received holy spirit from God as a gift to dwell inside him forever, just as Jesus had promised. The Apostles were filled with the gift of holy spirit and then spoke in tongues. After Pentecost, this spirit is given to everyone who confesses that Jesus is their Lord and believes that God raised him from the dead.

> "That if thou shalt confess with thy mouth the Lord Jesus, and shalt believe in thine heart that God hath raised him from the dead, thou shalt be saved" (Romans 10:9)

On the day of Pentecost, those present in the temple at Jerusalem heard the Apostles speak in tongues, even in their own native languages. But this was a phenomenon that they had never heard before. Then, they witnessed Peter standing up and boldly speaking about the crucifixion and resurrection of Jesus Christ. They were genuinely amazed at what had taken place. Many of those hearing these things turned to Peter and the other Apostles and said "men and brethren, what shall we do?" (Acts 2:37). Peter then addressed the crowd that had gathered:

"Then Peter said unto them, Repent and be baptised every one of you in the name of Jesus Christ for the remission of sins, and ye shall receive the gift of the Holy Ghost.

For the promise is unto you, and to your children, and to all that are afar off, *even* as many as the Lord our God shall call" (Acts 2:38-39)

The Word of God is simple: "Ye shall receive the gift". In legal terminology, the word "shall" is absolute and unequivocal. It cannot be broken. The gift of holy spirit is for everyone who confesses that Jesus Christ is their Lord and believes that God raised him from the dead. This is part of God's promise to everyone who has been called to Christ. Everyone who has believed that Jesus Christ is their Lord and that God has raised him from the dead receives this gift of holy spirit. Peter was speaking the Word of God. It is God's promise, not simply a promise emanating from man alone. The giving of holy spirit is God's work, not man's. When we confessed that Jesus is our Lord and believed that God raised him from the dead, He then imparted the gift of holy spirit to you and me also. We too have received the same gift of holy spirit that the Apostles received on the day of Pentecost.

Interestingly, when Peter spoke in Acts 2:38, he was actually referring to receiving the gift of holy spirit into manifestation. The Greek word for receive here is *"lambano"* which means more than just receiving passively. Peter was referring to how the spirit is evidenced in the senses realm. The apostles had just spoke in tongues, which is one of the evidences of the presence of the gift of holy spirit in a person.

A gift to keep

Notice also that the gift of holy spirit is actually called a "gift". Therefore, God imparts holy spirit to us as a gift. A gift is something for us to have and to keep. Remember, Jesus said that it would dwell in us forever – therefore, you and I will have this gift forever. This is significant in understanding the Great Secret because, as this gift becomes ours, it really means that the spirit that God gives us actually becomes our spirit. Paul wrote to the Christians in Rome and made reference to the gift of holy spirit becoming "our spirit":

"The Spirit [i.e. *God*] itself beareth witness with our spirit [i.e. *the gift in us*], that we are the children of God" (Romans 8:16)

So in this verse, we see that the gift has become "our spirit". God has given it to us as a gift. Therefore, as it is now our spirit, it will be with us forever. This is our true identity in Christ. It is in us right now and will remain in us as our spirit. God gave it to us on a forever basis. He will not take it from you.

"For the gifts and calling of God are without repentance." (Romans 11:29)

The phrase "without repentance" means that God will not change His mind after He has made this gift to you. In the Old Testament, David could ask God not to take his holy spirit from him. The reason for this is simply that God had never given the spirit to David as a gift. Rather, it was conditional upon David's faithfulness. However, God has imparted the holy spirit to you and I as a gift. The condition has already been fulfilled by the work of Jesus Christ and you have believed that he is your Lord and that God raised him from the dead. So today, He will not change His mind and take back His gift of holy spirit from you. Jesus did not lie when he said it would abide with us forever. He knew it would be a gift from the Father not because we deserve it but rather because we need it. Such is the love of God and the beautiful simplicity of His Word. Don't let anybody ever tell you that God can take it away from you. People who say such things are not sent from God.

The gift of holy spirit is yours. God has given it to you. To truly understand the riches of the glory of the Great Secret, you need to be absolutely convinced that the gift of holy spirit remains within you. And not only so, but also, that it has now become your spirit. It is God's gift to you. It is yours.

> "To whom God would make known what are the riches of the glory of this mystery among the Gentiles, which is Christ in you the hope of glory" (Colossians 1:27)

Christ is in you because you have the gift of holy spirit dwelling in you. And this spirit of Christ has now become your spirit.

Chapter 17: Born from above

What does being born again really mean?

When a person receives the gift of holy spirit for the first time, he is actually receiving the spirit of Christ. This is the gift. At this point, God saves that person. To understand this more clearly, we need to firstly understand that it is at this point we become a new born babe in Christ. This does not refer to a person of the flesh but rather a person of the spirit. Jesus began to explain this to Nicodemus but he struggled to understand it and he did not receive the witness from Jesus Christ.

"There was a man of the Pharisees, named Nicodemus, a ruler of the Jews:

The same came to Jesus by night, and said unto him, Rabbi, we know thou art a teacher come from God: for no man can do these miracles that thou doest, except God be with him.

Jesus answered and said unto him, Verily, verily, I say unto thee, Except a man be born again, he cannot see the kingdom of God.

Nicodemus saith unto him, How can a man be born when he is old? Can he enter the second time into his mother's womb, and be born?

Jesus answered, Verily, verily, I say unto thee, Except a man be born of water and *of* the Spirit, he cannot enter into the kingdom of God

That which is born of the flesh is flesh; and that which is born of the Spirit is spirit.

Marvel not that I said unto thee, Ye must be born again.

The wind bloweth where it listeth, and thou hearest the sound thereof, but canst not tell whence it cometh, and whither it goeth: so is everyone that is born of the Spirit.

Nicodemus answered and said unto him, How can these things be?

Jesus answered and said unto him, Art thou a master of Israel, and knowest not these things?

Verily, verily, I say unto thee, We speak that we do know, and testify that we have seen; and ye receive not our witness.

If I have told you earthly things, and ye believe not, how shall ye believe, if I tell you *of* heavenly things?" (John3:1-12)

Jesus said to Nicodemus that "Ye must be born again". The word "again" in the Greek texts is "*anothen*" which literally means "from above". Jesus Christ was saying that to see and enter the kingdom of God a man must be born from above. This is different from being born from the womb of your earthly mother. Jesus refers to a person's earthly birth when he speaks of being "born of water". Before a child's birth, the mother's waters break and the babe is then born. However, Jesus then went on to speak of a second birth which is from above; that is, being "born of the Spirit". This refers to being born from above by God himself.

It is God who begets you as a new born babe, not made of flesh but rather created in spirit. That which is born of the flesh (earthly mother) is flesh (a physical babe), but that which is born of the Spirit (God) is spirit (a new spiritual babe). This new spiritual babe is born from above (*Gr. "anothen"* which means from above or from the very top). The new spiritual babe is

63

begotten by God himself as His workmanship created in Christ. Paul refers to this in Ephesians

"For by grace are ye saved through faith; and that not of yourselves: it *is* the gift of God...... For we are his workmanship created in Christ Jesus..." (Ephesians 2:8,10a)

We are new born spiritual babes. We are God's workmanship not simply man's workmanship. This new born babe is created in Christ Jesus and we receive it in the gift of holy spirit.

As newborn babes

Very simply, we have no difficulty in understanding that a physical babe is just a babe and not a fully developed person. Likewise, when we were born again or born from above by God, we did not immediately grow into spiritual adulthood. Therefore, after being born again, we are encouraged to feed on the Word of God so that we may all grow up:

"As newborn babes, desire the sincere milk of the word, that ye may grow thereby" (I Peter 2:2)

By feeding on the Word of God we learn how to walk spiritually and grow up. There is another record in Peter which explains that the Christ in us is an incorruptible seed. Like a physical seed that will eventually spring forth into a shoot, and then a tree with branches to bear fruit and grow tall, so is the seed of Christ in us, except we will produce spiritual fruit. The word incorruptible refers to the perfection of Christ in that he is alive for evermore and cannot die. He is sinless.

"Being born again, not of corruptible seed, but of incorruptible by the word of God, which liveth and abideth for ever." (I Peter 1:23)

The phrase born again is "*anagennao*" in the Greek texts. This is a compound of two Greek words "*ana*" which means "up and again" and "*gennao*" which means to be born, to conceive, or to beget. Each born again believer is a new born babe who has been created in Christ; this is received by the imparting of the gift of holy spirit, which is incorruptible seed.

We have been born again so that we can see the things of God and enter His kingdom. Because we have the spirit in us, we can now discern the "deep things of God" which are the glorious riches of the Great Secret.

Chapter 18: Born again as the sons of God

Sons of God

We have already seen that we are God's very own workmanship created in Christ Jesus from incorruptible seed. We know that we have been born again by the Word of our God. This makes us God's sons by spiritual birth. The Word of God teaches us that when we received the gift of holy spirit we became the spiritual sons of God.

> "For ye have not received the spirit of bondage again to fear; but ye have received the Spirit of adoption, whereby we cry, Abba, Father." (Romans 8:15)

The word "adoption" in Romans 8:15 is a weak translation of the Greek word "*huiothesia*" which literally means sonship. God has worked in us something much more than simple adoption. He has begotten us as new babes born directly of His spirit. We have become the spiritual sons of God by His will. Do you consider yourself as a son of the Almighty God? The word of God declares that you are:

> "Behold what manner of love the Father hath bestowed upon us, that we should be called the sons of God: therefore the world knoweth us not, because it knew him not.
>
> Beloved, now are we the sons of God..." (I John 3:1-2a)

Today, you and I are the sons of God. Right now, we are His beloved family of sons who have been born from above.

> "The Spirit itself beareth witness with our spirit, that we are the children of God" (Romans 8:16)

Just take a few moments to think what a great privilege it is for you to be called a son by the Almighty God Himself.

It is Christ in you

The gift of holy spirit that we received is a sonship spirit. It is the spirit of the Son of God, Jesus Christ.

> ".... God sent forth His son.....that we might receive the adoption of sons. And because ye are sons, God hath sent forth the spirit of His son in to your hearts, crying, Abba, Father.
>
> Wherefore, thou art no more a servant, but a son; and if a son, then an heir of God through Christ." (Galatians 4:4-7)

Not everyone in the world today is a son of God – only those who have the spirit of Christ in them.

> "... Now if any man have not the Spirit of Christ, he is none of his." (Romans 8:9)

Christ is in us so we belong to Christ and the family of God.

> "Examine yourselves, whether ye be in the faith; prove your own selves, how that Jesus Christ is in you, except ye be reprobates?" (2 Corinthians 13:5)

We are sons of God today because we have the spirit of His son Jesus Christ in us. God declares that there are glorious riches to be found in the Christ in us.

> "To whom God would make known what are the riches of the glory of this mystery among the Gentiles, which is Christ in you the hope of glory" (Colossians 1:27)

All the treasures of wisdom and knowledge are hid in the Christ who is in us. We have been born again as the sons of God.

Chapter 19: More about the Great Secret of the Christ in you

Every spiritual blessing in Christ

There is a lot for us to learn about the spirit of Christ that God has placed within us. Firstly, it is His will that we are to desire the milk of the Word so that we may grow thereby. He wants us to know what He has made us to be in Christ. When we received the spirit in us, we also received everything in that spirit that God has made Christ to be unto us. God tells us that He has blessed us with every spiritual blessing in Christ,

> "Blessed *be* the God and Father of our Lord Jesus Christ, who hath blessed us with all spiritual blessings in heavenly *places* in Christ" (Ephesians 1:3)

What does this really mean? Well, there are many riches that belong to us in Christ. The more we grow in Christ, the more we will learn what these riches are. In this chapter we shall look at a few of these riches that are ours in Christ. In the rest of the book, we will discover more of these riches.

The Spirit of Christ in you is eternal life

Jesus Christ is alive and will be forever more. After being raised by our Father he cannot die ever again. This is the Christ who is alive in us. The spirit that we received from our Father is eternal life because death has no dominion whatsoever over Christ. So you can understand now that it is the spirit of the victorious Christ is in us today.

> "And if Christ *be* in you, the body *is* dead because of sin; but the spirit *is* life because of righteousness." (Romans 8:10)

The spirit in us is life because of God's righteousness. In His own righteous response to the death of His Son, God raised Jesus Christ up from the dead. Now the spirit of His ascended Son lives in you and me, and that spirit cannot die.

> "And this is the record, that God hath given to us eternal life, and this life is in his Son.
>
> He that hath the Son hath life; *and* he that hath not the Son of God hath not life.
>
> These things have I written unto you that believe on the name of the Son of God; that ye may know that ye have eternal life, and that ye may believe on the name of the Son of God." (I John 5:11-13)

We know that we have eternal life and this life is in his Son Jesus Christ who lives in us. It is eternal life in us because Christ is alive and will die no more. And we have his spirit in us as a gift from God.

You have been made the righteousness of God in him

All of what we have in Christ is by grace. This means that we didn't deserve it. But by God's righteous work and His own kindness we have Christ in us as a gift.

> "For He hath made him *to be* sin for us, who knew no sin; that we might be made the righteousness of God in him." (2 Corinthians 5:21)

It is astounding that you and I are made into the righteousness of God. That our righteousness is God's standard of righteousness, not man's. If God had not recorded this in His Word, I would have found it difficult to believe. Nevertheless, God knows exactly what He is saying. The spirit we have in us is from God and is righteous, holy and perfect.

"But of him are ye in Christ Jesus, who of God is made unto us wisdom, and righteousness, and sanctification, and redemption" (I Corinthians 1:30)

Because of the spirit in us, we now have God's redemption, sanctification and righteousness also in us. God's wisdom has been wrought in our lives, in our very beings. The Christ in us is perfect, holy and righteous. This is the very spirit that we have been given. And we know that it has become our spirit.

Do you know that the spirit in you cannot sin?

"We know that whosoever is born of God sinneth not; but he that is begotten of God keepeth himself, and that the wicked one toucheth him not" (I John 5:18).

The Christ in you is born of God and is perfect and cannot sin. This verse refers to the spiritual man, not the fleshly man.

New man and new nature

When we were born again or rather born from above, we became a person created in spirit. This is our Father's own workmanship. God calls this the new man:

"And that ye put on the new man, which after God is created in righteousness and true holiness." (Ephesians 4:24)

The new man is the Christ in you. It has been created in righteousness and true holiness. It is Christ's eyes behind your eyes; it is Christ's hands behind your hands; it is Christ's feet behind your feet; it is Christ, the spiritual man in you, born of the Father. This new man has a new nature. It is the nature of God in Christ in you. Through this work of God we became partakers of the divine nature.

"Whereby are given unto us exceeding great and precious promises that by these ye might be partakers of the divine nature, having escaped the corruption that is in the world through lust." (2 Peter 1:4)

This knowledge of the new man being a partaker of the divine nature is at the very heart of the Great Secret in Christ. To walk in this secret, we need to be convinced that God has created us in Christ as a new man. That new man maybe just a babe but we are about to grow up. The walk of power, love and glory that is in Christ is not a walk of the flesh but rather it is a walk of the spirit. It is the new man walking. This is at the very heart of what God has made us to be in Christ. He has begotten us by incorruptible seed. He has created us afresh in Christ as a spiritual man. In this, we are His workmanship. It is "Christ in you the hope of glory".

The new man is righteous, perfect and holy. It is sinless and cannot sin because it is the incorruptible seed of "Christ in you".

Chapter 20: Walking in the spirit

Walking in the new life in us

God has certainly placed something great in us. We have seen how He has begotten us spiritually as His sons. He has brought us into a new birth with opportunities for living in a new way. We have been created as a new man made of spirit in Christ. How perfect His workmanship truly is. We know that the spirit is life because Christ was raised from the dead and is alive forever more. And this is how we have eternal life abiding in us.

The Apostle Paul wrote to the Christians in Galatia telling them that they had been made alive in the spirit; therefore, it is logical that all Christians should now walk in that spirit:

> "If we live in the spirit, let us also walk in the spirit."
> (Galatians 5:25)

To walk in the spirit means that we are to walk in the new life that our Father has placed in us. This is a learning process just like an earthly babe is physically alive at birth and then learns to move and then crawl and eventually walks. As spiritual babes, we are first made alive in Christ. Then, we learn to take our first steps walking spiritually with the Christ in us. How beautiful is God's will for His children.

Overcoming sin with the Christ in us

One of the great promises in God's Word is that if we walk in the spirit, which is walking in our new man, we shall overcome the weaknesses and failures of our flesh. We can overcome sin.

> "*This* I say then, Walk in the spirit, and ye shall not fulfil the lust of the flesh." (Galatians 5:16)

If we walk in the spirit, we shall not sin. The reason for this is that the strength of Christ is greater than sin and death. This greater strength is at work in the spirit of Christ in us. We have access into this greatness simply when we walk in the Christ in us.

"*There* is therefore now no condemnation to them that are in Christ Jesus, who walk not after the flesh, but after the spirit. For the law of the spirit of life in Christ Jesus hath made me free from the law of sin and death." (Romans 8:1-2)

Christ is free from sin and death. Christ now lives in us and leads us to victory. The law of life in Christ is greater than the law of sin and death.

Counting the old man dead

Paul spoke of "being made conformable unto his death" (Philippians 3:10) so that he could walk in the new life that is in Christ. What this really means is that he died to himself so that he could be devoted to the Christ in him, which is far greater. He would rather live the new life of the Christ in him, than continue in his own old nature.

"Know ye not, that so many of us as were baptised into Jesus Christ were baptised into his death?

Therefore, we are buried with him by baptism into death: that like as Christ was raised up from the dead by the glory of the Father, even so we also should walk in newness of life." (Romans 6:3-4)

Finding our new life in Christ

Remember what God says about our walk:

"For we walk by faith not by sight" (2 Corinthians 5:7).

Father has promised a new life for us today in Christ. To find this new life that God has placed in us we have to do two things. Firstly, we must die to our old nature. Secondly, we must set our hearts and minds on the promises of God about the new nature that is now in us.

> "Likewise reckon ye also yourselves to be dead indeed unto sin, but alive unto God through Jesus Christ our Lord" (Romans 6:11)

We are to yield ourselves, not to our old nature, but rather unto God who is the Father of our new nature. God has promised us new life in Christ and He will not fail to meet us at this junction. We know that the law of the spirit of life has set us free from the law of sin and death. So the life we find in Christ is greater and more powerful than sin and death. So we set our hearts on God's promises and He meets us there with the abundant life in Christ.

> "For to be carnally minded *is* death, but to be spiritually minded *is* life and peace." (Romans 8:6)

God leads us into this life as we set our hearts and minds on His Word. If we follow our old nature, we will walk into death. If we trust God, that the law of the spirit of life is indeed greater and leads us to our new life in Christ, then we shall surely live. Trusting God in this way means we walk out on His Word and prove its faithfulness.

> "For if ye shall live after the flesh, ye shall die: but if ye through the spirit do mortify the deeds of the body, ye shall live." (Romans 8:13)

Walking in the spirit will actually mortify the deeds of the old nature. Mortify means to put to death. Our old nature can be simply displaced by something that is greater and more powerful... the Christ in us. This is to be our mindset.

Paul wrote to the Galatians that he lived the Christ in him:

> "I am crucified with Christ: nevertheless I live; yet not I, but Christ liveth in me: and the life which I now live in the flesh I live by the faith of the Son of God, who loved me, and gave himself for me." (Galatians 2:20)

That's where every Christian ought to be! Walking by faith is literally walking upon the written Word. We need to learn what the Word says about our walk in Christ. In particular, we should seek that which is addressed directly to us in the Church Epistles. We are to mind the things of the spirit.

> "Brethren, be followers together of me, and mark them which walk so as ye have us for an ensample." (Philippians 3:17)

Walking in the spirit is walking by faith. It is a walk of believing God's Word, and in particular we are to believe what God says about the new man. As we take each step in that wonderful Word, we are walking in the Christ in us; we are walking in the very life that is in Christ. We are living the Word.

The rule that only the new man counts for anything in Christ

In Christ, there is a rule that only the new nature has any worth and all things of the flesh are of no profit. Peace and mercy from God are upon all Christians who walk according to this rule. As far as man and this world are concerned, the Word of God declares that everything outside of Christ is dead and of no spiritual profit. Understanding that you are a new creation in Christ is required before you can really understand the Great Secret. Indeed, the Great Secret is built upwards from the new creation.

"But God forbid that I should glory, save in the cross of our Lord Jesus Christ, by whom the world is crucified unto me, and I unto the world.

For in Christ Jesus neither circumcision availeth anything, nor uncircumcision, but a new creature.

And as many as walk according to this rule, peace *be* on them, and mercy…"(Galatians 6:14-16a)

All else is dead. Only the new born again spiritual man is accepted by God. In Christ, there is a rule that only the new man is of any worth – all else is worthless. This is one of the rules that God has declared that we are to walk by. The Great Secret is about our new nature, the new man which God has created in Christ. The Great Secret is opened up and revealed in the new man. This understanding will help us to walk by the spirit in all of the greatness of the secret in Christ.

Chapter 21: The preaching of the Cross and the Great Secret (Part One)

The Cross is the power and wisdom of God

I would like to show you the meaning of the crucifixion with regards to the Great Secret. Remember the secret had been hid in God and was not revealed until after Pentecost. In the same manner, there are truths about the 'cross' of our Lord Jesus Christ that were also hidden and not fully revealed until after Pentecost because they form part of the Great Secret. In this chapter we shall look at these truths.

Firstly, Paul, the Apostle of the Great Secret, wrote to the Corinthians telling them that the preaching of the 'cross' is the power and wisdom of God:

> "For Christ sent me not to baptize, but to preach the gospel: not with wisdom of words, lest the cross of Christ should be made of none effect.
>
> For the preaching of the cross is to them that perish foolishness; but unto us which are saved it is the power of God.
>
> But we preach Christ crucified, unto the Jews a stumbling block, and unto the Greeks foolishness;
>
> But unto them which are called, both Jews and Greeks, Christ the power of God, and the wisdom of God."
> (1 Corinthians 1:17, 18, 23, 24)

To many, the idea of the 'cross' is utter foolishness, but for us who are saved it is the power and wisdom of God. In this chapter we will look at this wisdom and power. There is much to learn about the significance of the 'cross' to us.

The Greek word for 'cross' in the Bible is *"stauros"*. In a physical sense, it means a stake or a post upon which crucifixion takes place as a punishment for a crime committed. In the Eastern culture at the time of Jesus Christ's death, it was considered to be the most humiliating form of death. Instead of dying peacefully in honour, it was the most shameful way to die.

The 'cross' of our Lord Jesus Christ refers to the actual stake upon which he was crucified. Yet, there are deeper meanings of this 'cross' which show the power and wisdom of God.

We glory in the cross

It is astounding that the Lord Jesus Christ, who came to mankind in love and performing the great works of God, should be killed by the religious and political rulers of this world. Yet this happened. Jesus Christ is pure and undefiled but this world is evil and impure. The Apostle Paul considered that through the cross of our Lord Jesus Christ the world had been crucified to him and he also had been crucified to the world:

> "But God forbid that I should glory, save in the cross of our Lord Jesus Christ, by whom the world is crucified unto me, and I unto the world
>
> For in Christ Jesus neither circumcision availeth any thing, nor uncircumcision, but a new creature." (Galatians 6:14-15)

Paul gloried in the 'cross' of our Lord Jesus Christ. What this really meant was that as far as this world is concerned Paul considered everything in it as dead and of no profit. He died to this world and was showing the Galatians that there is nothing godly which belongs to this world. In contrast, the new creation which is the new man, has worth. The new man was created by

God in righteousness and true holiness. Instead of glorying in the flesh and the things of this world, Paul would glory in the 'cross' of our Lord Jesus Christ which shows that the things in the world have no true glory. The 'cross' decimates the proud claims of this world.

God says that this world is dead

The Bible says that this world is already dead:

> "For the love of Christ constraineth us; because we thus judge, that if one died for all, then were all dead." (2 Corinthians 5:14)

The word constraineth here is like God putting a 'straight jacket' of discernment upon us so that we would be made free. The love of God in Christ fixes our discernment telling us Jesus Christ came to taste death for every person because every person was dead already. Man, without the work of the Lord Jesus Christ, does not have eternal life abiding in him. Without Christ man is also spiritually dead to God and has no living relationship with Him.

Therefore, to glory in the 'cross' of our Lord Jesus Christ is to say that the world has no true honour or value to you; that it is dead both because it cannot offer you eternal life; and that in the world mankind is spiritually dead to God. Therefore, by the 'cross' of our Lord Jesus Christ we are shown that the world is crucified and made dead unto us, and that we too died to this world.

Our association with Christ

Jesus Christ associated himself with us so that we could share in his death, resurrection, ascension and heavenly life. This sharing is fully available today and is at the heart of the gospel of the Great Secret in Christ which Paul preached.

"Buried with him in baptism wherein also ye are risen with *him* through the faith of the operation of God, who hath raised him from the dead." (Colossians 2:12)

In Christ we died both to the deadness of this world and also to ourselves so that we could be made alive instead in the new man and in the riches of the glory of the Great Secret.

"Know ye not, that so many of us as were baptized into Jesus Christ were baptized into his death?

Therefore we are buried with him by baptism into death: that like as Christ was raised up from the dead by the glory of the Father, even so we should walk in newness of life.

For if we have been planted together in the likeness of his death, we shall be also *in the likeness of his* resurrection" (Romans 6:3-5).

In the cross of our Lord Jesus Christ, we all died so that we could go on to share in the power of his resurrection. This is the wisdom and power of the 'cross' of our Lord Jesus Christ; having died with Christ, God could then quicken us to be made alive again as he made Jesus Christ alive again from the dead. Jesus Christ led the way before us. Clearly, we did not die with Christ in a physical sense because we are still alive in our flesh. Paul explains that it was our old man which was crucified with Christ.

"Knowing this, that our old man is crucified with *him*, that the body of sin might be destroyed that henceforth we should not serve sin.

For he that is dead is freed from sin.

Now if we be dead with Christ, we believe that we shall also live with him" (Romans 6:6-8).

The old man is not the new born again spiritual man but rather it is the nature of Adam which is in every person. This nature is sinful. It is the nature that every man has. In contrast, we know that our new born again man is spiritual, born of God and is righteous and perfect. In the sonship spirit that we have from God, we cannot sin. However, the old man is the man of the flesh and the way of the old man is sin. Paul said that we are to count this flesh man as dead, as having been crucified with Christ upon the 'cross'. Jesus Christ died to redeem us from all the sinful imperfections that are part of our nature as fallen mankind. He took them upon himself when he died on the cross. Therefore, we die to our old nature that we may live our new nature which is Christ:

> "I am [*was*] crucified with Christ: nevertheless I live; yet not I, but Christ liveth in me: and the life which I now live in the flesh I live by the faith of the Son of God, who loved me, and gave himself for me." (Galatians 2:20)

The significance of the 'cross' to the Great Secret

Part of the significance of the 'cross' to the Great Secret is that we are made conformable to the death of Jesus Christ so that we may live in the life of Christ.

> "That I may know him, and the power of his resurrection, and the fellowship of his sufferings, being made conformable unto his death" (Philippians 3:10).

Instead of living according to this world, we die to this world by being made conformable to the cross. God has appointed us to live the glorious riches of the Great Secret which are greater and more powerful than anything that this world can offer:

"Always bearing about in the body the dying of our Lord Jesus, that the life also of Jesus might be made manifest in our body.

For we which live are alway delivered unto death for Jesus' sake, that the life also of Jesus might be manifest in our body." (2 Corinthians 4:10-11)

Jesus Christ came and identified himself with mankind. Man was spiritually dead and would physically die to be no more. Jesus Christ came to redeem us on both counts.

For us who are saved, we are with Christ in his death but we are also with Christ in his life because Father raised him from the dead. We die daily to ourselves so that the life of Jesus Christ can be made manifest in us.

Enemies of the Cross of Christ

We know that Jesus Christ came to die for the sins of all mankind, but there is a verse in Philippians that speaks of the enemies of the cross of Christ:

"For many walk, of whom I have told you often, and now tell you even weeping, *that they are* the enemies of the cross of Christ" (Philippians 3:18)

The "many" that Paul was speaking of were the carnally minded Christians who, after receiving Christ in them and dying to the world, returned to the world to continue as before. Therefore, they were treading underfoot the death of our Lord Jesus Christ and making a mockery of the cross. The end of that behaviour is destruction. However, for us who truly belong to Christ by way of us walking in him, we can say:

"And they that are Christ's have crucified the flesh with the affections and lusts. " (Galatians 5:24).

Part VI - The Great Secret of Growing Up Into Christ

Chapter 22: The heart of the Great Secret

It is a wonderful thing to have come this far in understanding and seeing the Word of God unfold before our very eyes. However, I feel that up until now, we have only just scratched the surface of what the Great Secret is really all about. The next sections will open up to us the depths of God's heart concerning our part in this secret. You will come to understand what He has called us to in a much more meaningful way than ever before.

The Almighty God, our Father, has called us to be conformed to the image of Christ:

> "For whom He did foreknow, he also did predestinate *to be* conformed to the image of his Son, that he might be the first born among many brethren." (Romans 8:29-30)

The words "conformed to the image of His son" mean that our Father will fashion us into Christ. He will nurture you and I in the Great Secret so that we look like Christ spiritually on the inside, in our hearts. It is God Himself who performs this work in us so that we begin to walk like Christ, speak like him and think like him, even today. This is His will for us. God wants us to grow up into Christ in all things.

> "But speaking the truth in love, may grow up into him in all things, which is the head, *even* Christ" (Ephesians 4:15)

This growing up into Christ is at the very heart of the Great Secret. It is the heartbeat of God's will for us today. It is the Father working with His children, bringing us up to walk as the glorious sons of God. He will teach us marvellous things as we sit at His feet, receiving the greatness of His Word.

"To walk as he walks, to think as he thinks, to speak what he speaks, to live as he lives.

Great news,

We will smile as he smiles, and we will love as he loves,

We will pray as he prays, and we will bless as he blesses,

We have his joy and we will rejoice as he does,

We will shine as he shines, in the very same radiance,

We belong to the same family,

Because of him, we are the sons of the living God

And we are being fashioned into the same image"

This is the Great Secret.

Chapter 23: The image of God and the image of the Devil

There are two images for mankind. Man will either be conformed to the image of God or the image of the Devil.

Adam in the image and likeness of God

God's heart has always been for man to have fellowship with Him and so He originally created man in His own image and likeness for this purpose.

> And God said, Let us make man in our image, after our likeness........
>
> So God created man in his *own* image, in the image of God created he him; male and female created he them. (Genesis 1:26-27)

The image and likeness of God are both spiritual and holy in nature. But, Adam was given spirit from God upon a condition that he must not eat of the tree of knowledge of good and evil.

> "And the LORD God commanded the man, saying, Of every tree of the garden thou mayest freely eat:
>
> But of the tree of the knowledge of good and evil, thou shalt not eat of it: for in the day that thou eatest thereof thou shalt surely die." (Genesis 2:16-17)

The giving of the spirit from God allowed perfect communication between God, who is Spirit and Holy, and Adam, who was human but had been given holy spirit. However, in eating of the tree of knowledge of good and evil Adam blatantly disobeyed

God. This was despite being told that "in the day that thou eatest thereof thou shall surely die" (Genesis 2:17). In the very day that Adam disobeyed this conditional agreement with God, Adam died. However, he did not immediately die in a physical sense but rather he died spiritually there and then, in the very day that God had told him he would. Adam had lost the spirit which had been given to him upon a condition.

In the Bible, the absence of the spirit from God is called death. From God's perspective, a person without the spirit of God is dead just like from man's perspective a person without breath life is physically dead. Before we received the spirit from God, we were dead in sins following the ways of the devil:

> "And you *hath he quickened*, who were dead in trespasses and sins;
>
> Wherein time past ye walked according to the course of this world, according to the prince of the power of the air, the spirit that now worketh in the children of disobedience" (Ephesians 2:1-2)

The prince of the power of the air is the Adversary, the Devil. At one time, we all walked according to his direction. The Word of God also tells us that we were once dead (spiritually) like all of mankind.

> "For the love of Christ constraineth us; because we thus judge, that if one died for all, then were all dead" (2 Corinthians 5:14)

But when we received the gift of holy spirit from God, we became alive again to God. This is what Paul was referring to when he said that we were quickened which means to be made alive:

"Even when we were dead in sins, hath quickened us together with Christ (by grace ye are saved)" (Ephesians 2:5)

Except for those in Christ, all mankind today are dead in God's eyes and are without holy spirit. Moreover, not only is man dead today, but it is worse still in that man is unknowingly being conformed into the image of the Devil in this spiritual deadness.

Man in the image and likeness of the Devil

From the moment Adam had lost the spirit, man was no longer in the image of God. It is a grave error to think that all of unsaved mankind is in the image of God today. Nothing could be farther from the real truth. The wars, the fighting, the selfishness, the greed, the strife, the unsound mind, the envies, the idolatry, the lack of respect – all these belong to the carnal nature of man. They are not works according to the image of God.

Since Eden, man has lived in a fallen state and has not been conformed into the image of God who is Holy and Spirit. Moreover, today man is being conformed to the ways of the world. This is actually being fashioned into the image of the Adversary, the Devil, who is called the god of this world.

"But if our gospel be hid, it is hid to them that are lost:

In whom the god of this world hath blinded the minds of them which believe not, lest the light of the glorious gospel of Christ, who is the image of God, should shine unto them." (2 Corinthians 4:3-4)

As "the god of this world", the Adversary governs it with the rule of evil. The system of things has been developed in the image of the Adversary, the Devil:

"*And* we know that we are of God and the whole world lieth in wickedness." (1 John 5:19)

The phrase "lieth in wickedness" refers to what has been conformed to the image of the Adversary.

"Love not the world, neither the things *that are* in the world. If any man love the world, the love of the Father is not in him.

For all that *is* in the world, the lust of the flesh, and the lust of the eyes, and the pride of life, is not of the Father, but is of the world.

And the world passeth away and the lust thereof"
(1 John 2:15-17a).

Today, unsaved man is being conformed into the image of the Devil. Man is following the Adversary into perdition.

Jesus Christ came to change all this and save us from this fallen nature. Jesus Christ came to restore man's broken relationship with God. Through Christ, God has made us alive again and has delivered us from the ways of the Adversary.

"Who hath delivered us from the power of darkness, and hath translated *us* into the kingdom of his dear Son:

In whom we have redemption through his blood, *even* the forgiveness of sins:

Who is the image of the invisible God..."
(Colossians 1:13-15a)

If a man accepts Jesus Christ as his Lord, then he no longer has to be conformed to this world. He is given a new direction. He can now be conformed to the image of Christ, who is both the Son of God and the image of God.

Chapter 24: The mind of Christ and the Great Secret

Man's carnal mind cannot comprehend the Great Secret. However, the mind of Christ holds the Great Secret in all its glory, wisdom and depth.

Perfect in spirit, imperfect in mind

When God brought us into our new birth, we received His perfection within us. However, that perfection is all wrapped up in the spirit of Christ which we received at that time. The Word of God also calls this spirit of Christ in us the "incorruptible seed" and "the gift of holy spirit".

At that point, we were perfect in spirit but our minds were for the most part still carnal. We had not yet developed spiritual minds. Our thoughts, our mental patterns and indeed the whole life of our minds were all still fashioned after the pattern of our old fallen nature.

Hence, there is now a conflict in us: we are perfect in spirit but imperfect in our minds. Although our spirit is perfect, the way we think is not yet fully in accordance with God's heart. The good news is that our Father wants to help us make our minds new, to be fashioned after His mind and after His thinking. The Word of God declares that it is available today for us to have the mind of Christ. In this chapter, we are going to explore how our loving Father makes it available for the mind of Christ to be developed in us.

Be not conformed to this world, but be ye transformed

The mind of man is far different from the mind of Christ. We have seen how unsaved man is being fashioned into the image of the Adversary. Today, man has an unsound mind, but God tells all of us who are in Christ that our minds can be made new. This is done when the Word of God dwells in us which is putting God's thoughts in our minds. Then our hearts will be transformed:

> "And be not conformed to this world: but be ye transformed by the renewing of your mind, that ye may prove what *is* that good, and acceptable, and perfect, will of God."
> (Romans 12:2)

The word transformed is *"metamorphoo"* which literally means to be changed. Our Father will help us renew the working patterns of our minds through the power of His Word and then our hearts will become transformed. The word mind here is the Greek work *"nous"* which refers to the whole organ of the mind. This is to be made new. The newness is a result of the power of the Word of God. It is God Himself who fulfils His Word in us.

God wants you to have the mind of Christ

Paul wrote to the Corinthians telling them that those who had grown up in Christ had the mind of Christ.

> "For who hath known the mind of the Lord, that he should instruct him? But we have the mind of Christ."
> (1 Corinthians 2:16)

The "we" of verse 16 does not refer to the carnally minded Corinthians to whom Paul could not yet declare the Great Secret. Rather, in the context, it refers to "the perfect" or the mature in Christ spoken of in verse 6.

"Howbeit we speak wisdom among them that are perfect: yet not the wisdom of this world, nor of the princes of this world, that come to nought" (1 Corinthians 2:6)

The majority of the Corinthian believers were still carnal and not yet spiritual in their minds. They were still walking in their old ways, the same as they had done for many years prior to being saved. However, Paul and the other believers of verse 6 were being perfected in their minds. They were putting on Christ in their minds,

"But put ye on the Lord Jesus Christ and make not provision for the flesh, to *fulfil* the lusts *thereof*." (Romans 13:14)

Putting on the Lord Jesus Christ refers to the mind of Christ which is a perfect mind and is in total alignment with God's will. The pattern of Christ's mind is actually the Word of God. The thoughts of Christ's mind are the thoughts of the Word. Simply put, the Christ mind thinks the Word of God. Your mind is changed into the mind of Christ when the Word of God dwells in your mind and heart richly.

Paul later wrote to Timothy that within the spirit that we have received is one of a sound mind.

"For God hath not given us the spirit of fear; but of power, and of love, and of a sound mind." (2 Timothy 1:7)

This sound mind that Paul was referring to is the mind of Christ. The soundness of this mind is the very soundness of God Himself.

The Word of God is the will of God

It is a great revelation to the heart of any humble believer that the Word of God is actually the will of God. To know God's will, we have to go to the Bible which is the book of life. The words of God are the very thoughts of God. These words declare unto us

His will. His promises to us are His will. What He has made us to be in Christ is His will. What He has told us that we can do with His power in us is His will. How He wants us to walk is His will for us. All of these things are declared in the Bible. Therefore, the Word of God is the will of God.

The Word of God is also the mind of God. When the Word of God becomes the prevalent thinking of our minds, we then have the mind of Christ. To do this we have to let the Word dwell in our minds richly. Then our minds will become fashioned after Christ's mind.

> "Let the word of Christ dwell in you richly in all wisdom......" Colossians 3:16).

Paul also prayed for the believers in Colossae that they "might be filled with the knowledge of his will in all wisdom and spiritual understanding" and that they would increase "in the knowledge of God" (Colossians 1:11 and 12). This is certainly something that God also desires for us. He will help us.

The thoughts of Jesus Christ

> "Let this mind be in you that was also in Christ Jesus" (Philippians 2:5)

The word mind in this verse is "*phronema*" which literally means thoughts. Therefore, we are to let these thoughts be in us which were in Christ Jesus. This is a clear instruction. We are to think like Christ. This is literally thinking the Word. We are to have the thoughts that Christ had.

The thoughts referred to here are the thoughts of God. The words of God are the very thoughts of God. These thoughts are higher than man's thoughts, and they are also of a different pattern to man's thoughts.

The higher thoughts

"For my thoughts *are* not your thoughts, neither *are* your ways my ways, saith the LORD.

 For *as* the heavens are higher than the earth, so are my ways higher than your ways, and my thoughts than your thoughts." (Isaiah 55:8-9)

God has given us His Word for this purpose: that our minds can think this Word which is God's thoughts. This is a wonderful privilege. Instead of our minds being occupied with man's thoughts, rather our minds can be filled with a higher thinking, the very thoughts of God himself. How sweet it is for us that we can think the way our Father thinks. He has made this wonderful opportunity available to us.

The life of the mind

"And be renewed in the spirit of your mind" (Ephesians 4:23)

The word spirit here is "*psuche*" and refers to the life of the mind. So far we have looked at the organ of the mind which holds the thoughts of the mind. These are to be made new by being fashioned after Christ. The life of the mind is also to be made new. This is something more. The organ of the mind and the thoughts of the mind determine what is the life of the mind. For us, the life of our minds is to be the new man which is Christ in us. All of this fits perfectly together in God's Word:

"And be renewed in the spirit of your mind;

And that ye put on the new man which after God is created in righteousness and true holiness" (Ephesians 4:23 - 24).

The new life of the mind is literally the life of the new man, which is the life of Christ.

Conclusion

Not only has our loving Father saved us by the new birth in Christ, in His wisdom He has also made the mind of Christ available to us. Our entire minds, our thoughts and the life of our minds can all be made new. The aim is for us to be conformed to Christ so that he dwells in our hearts. God has wrought perfection in us by placing the perfect spirit in us and is now making the perfect mind of Christ available to us if we follow His way. We have been called unto the perfect man of Christ Jesus:

> "Till we all come in the unity of the faith, and of the knowledge of the Son of God, unto a perfect man, unto the measure of the stature of the fulness of Christ" (Ephesians 4:13).

The revelation of the Great Secret is not for the carnal mind of man. It is the spiritual food of the new man. It is for the perfect mind of Christ. The mind of Christ is able to perfectly comprehend and understand the Great Secret.

Being transformed into Christ involves the renewing of our minds. The power of His Word will accomplish this. We will come to see that it is the Father lovingly nurturing His children to grow us all up into Christ in the "all things" that he is.

Chapter 25: The Great Secret of growing up into Christ – the image of God

Our calling – to be conformed to the image of Christ

God has called you and I to be conformed to the image of Christ.

> "For whom He did foreknow, he also did predestinate *to be* conformed to the image of his Son, that he might be the first born among many brethren." (Romans 8:29-30)

Whilst the rest of unsaved mankind is being conformed to this world, we are being conformed into the image of His Son. You and I were once dead. Now, today, we are being transformed into the very image of Christ as our minds are renewed.

> "And be not conformed to this world: but be ye transformed by the renewing of your mind, that ye may prove what *is* that good, and acceptable, and perfect, will of God."
> (Romans 12:1-2)

It is by the renewing of the mind that we are transformed into Christ. This transformation comes from the power of the Word of God that dwells in us. God holds the responsibility for the power of the Word and in this He is faithful. So, when we let the Word dwell in us richly, we are inviting our heavenly Father, the Almighty God to work in us.

> "For it is God which worketh in you both to will and to do of *his* good pleasure." (Philippians 2:13)

It is the power of God in the Word dwelling in our minds that causes us to be transformed into His Son. God is at work in nurturing His sons, and this work is in us, today.

Being changed into the same image

What a privilege it is to be changed into Christ. God works in us so that we will look like Christ on the inside, in our hearts. He has enabled us to walk like Christ walked. Paul illuminated the Corinthians with this powerful statement:

> "But we all, with open face beholding as in a glass the glory of the Lord, are changed into the same image from glory to glory, *even* as by the Spirit of the Lord." (2 Corinthians 3:18)

What a wonderful truth. God is changing the faithful today into the same image of Christ from one glory to another glory. Every change that our Father works in us is glorious because every aspect of Christ is glorious. Jesus Christ has been glorified and we are being changed into him. No wonder Paul was so eager to die to his own self so that he could win Christ.

> "Yea doubtless, and I count all things *but* loss for the excellency of the knowledge of Christ Jesus my Lord: for whom I have suffered the loss of all things, and do count them *but* dung, that I may win Christ" (Philippians 3:8).

To win Christ means to grow up into him. Paul had no space left in himself for anything that he had previously been when he did not know Christ. Paul would say that by Jesus Christ "the world is crucified unto me, and I unto the world" (Galatians 6:14). Everything that he was and stood for had died in Christ. He counted his standing as a Hebrew of Hebrews to be nothing more than dung, so that he could give that entire space over to Christ, to live the Christ in him instead.

> "I am crucified with Christ: nevertheless I live; yet not I, but Christ liveth in me: and the life which I now live in the flesh I live by the faith of the Son of God, who loved me, and gave himself for me." (Galatians 2:20)

To live by the faith of Jesus Christ means that we will live the Christ in us. This is walking in the new nature as the new man created by God in Christ. Considering that we were once dead in trespasses and sins, this calling of God to be changed into the image of Christ is a wonderful thing. God has called you and I to be changed into Christ.

Growing up into Christ in all things

Being changed into the same image is growing up into Christ in all things:

> "But speaking the truth in love, may grow up into him in all things, which is the head, *even* Christ" (Ephesians 4:15)

You and I, who were once unsaved, can now grow up into Christ himself. This is wonderful. The "in all things" of verse 15 are the all things of Christ - each aspect of Christ is glorious. Each step of growth that we take in Christ we are being changed from one glorious aspect of him into another glorious aspect of him. What wisdom is this that the Father has abounded towards us – it is truly great. It is the Great Secret in Christ that God had previously kept hid in Himself from all ages and generations but He has now revealed it in this Age of Grace. Today, we are growing up into Christ himself. We have been called to be conformed not to the image of this world but to the image of Christ.

The hope of His calling

In Ephesians, Paul prayed for the faithful in Christ:

> "The eyes of your understanding being enlightened; that ye may know what is the hope of his calling, and what the riches of the glory of his inheritance in the saints" (Ephesians 1:18)

The hope of his calling is that one day we will be made fully like Christ. The Word of God says that one day we shall be like him in every way:

> "Beloved, now are we the sons of God, and it doth not yet appear what we shall be: but we know that, when he shall appear, we shall be like him; for we shall see him as he is. (1 John 3:2)

In that day we will become "the stature of the fulness of Christ" (Ephesians 4:13). Today however, we are growing up in him. We have died to ourselves so that we can become what Christ is. We have been created as a new man in Christ by God our Father. The Almighty God has made this available through the loving obedience and sacrifice of Jesus Christ, His Son.

The image of God

Remember in Genesis 1:26-27, Father says let us make man in our likeness and image. The image and likeness of God refers to the spirit of God and the nature of God. As we know, man (Adam) lost spirit, and today man is in a fallen state. Today, unsaved man is not in the image of God but rather is being conformed to this world whose god is the Devil. Man is being conformed into the image of the Devil to varying degrees and all men have fallen short of the glory of the Father. But in Christ, Father has provided another way…the Great Secret that was kept hidden from before the founding of the world. In this Great Secret we become fashioned into Christ who is the very image of God.

> "Who is the image of the invisible God, the firstborn of every creature" (Colossians 1:15)

There is an even greater statement where Father says that Jesus Christ is the brightness of God's glory and the express image of His very person.

"Who being the brightness of *his* glory, and the express image of his person..." (Hebrews 1:3)

We are called to be fashioned, conformed, and patterned into the image of His son, Jesus Christ.

"For whom He did foreknow, he also did predestinate *to be* conformed to the image of his Son, that he might be the first born among many brethren." (Romans 8:29)

So, to follow this through, we are being changed into the image of Christ, who is the Son of God, who is the very image of God Himself and who is the brightness of God's own glory. This is at the heartbeat of the Great Secret.

The prize

The prize of this high calling of God in Christ is that one day, we will be fully like him in all that he is:

"I press toward the mark for the prize of the high calling of God in Christ Jesus." (Philippians 3:14)

One day, we will be fully grown up into him. However, we are pressing toward that mark being changed along the way into the all things that Jesus Christ is today. He is the ascended victorious living Christ.

Chapter 26: Renewed in *"epignosis"* according to the image of God

"Epignosis"

The Greek word *"epignosis"* is a key to the understanding the secret. It is used many times in the Epistles. The word is a component of two words: *"epi"* which means upon; and *"gnosis"* which means to know by experience. It is something more than mere head knowledge. Moreover, it refers to a position of knowledge that is acquired only when the subject matter has been experienced.

"Epignosis" is the knowledge that is full or mature, and in the Epistles specifically refers to the real knowledge of Christ found by those who have actually lived the secret of Christ in them.

In an earlier chapter, we have already seen that *"epignosis"* is the strongest word for knowledge in the Bible and refers to the full mature knowledge of the Great Secret in Christ. Having experienced the secret, a person would then be positioned upon (*"epi"*) that knowledge as having been matured by it. So, the Great Secret in Christ is for living, not merely for head knowledge. Therefore, we will really come to know the Great Secret as we believe what the Word of God says about it and then go on to live it in all its fulness. In our hearts, we then become what Christ is.

The Great Secret can only be truly known by actually living its truths which means coming to know them by experience. Such a walk requires faithfulness. To believe the Word means to abide by it or to actually do what it says. The theologians and the academics will never truly know the Great Secret in Christ unless they come to live it and thereby know it by experience. The Great

Secret is for living. God protects the jewels of the truth of the secret in this manner. However, such jewels can be reached by believing and walking in faithfulness.

Being renewed in "*epignosis*"

This true knowledge is so powerful that our new man is renewed in it. The word "renewed" here means to acquire a new quality and in particular this refers to us growing up more and more into Christ.

> "And have put on the new *man*, which is renewed in knowledge [*epignosis*] after the image of him that created him" (Colossians 3:10).

We grow up into the new man more and more through experientially knowing the Christ in us. The Word of God teaches us what God has made Christ to be unto us. And in believing and walking according to this Word, we come to know experientially what it is to live the Christ in us thereby manifesting more of Christ in who we are. For the faithful, this renewing occurs daily:

> "For which cause we faint not; but though our outward man perish, yet the inward *man* is renewed day by day." (2 Corinthians 4:16)

This renewing really means that we are growing up into him, so that the man of our heart is the Christ, the perfect man, the Son of God. The new quality that is becoming more manifest in our lives is the Christ who is the image of God Himself. Our new man grows in our hearts into this very image. This explains the latter part of this verse. Simply put, the more our new man grows in our hearts, the more of the quality of Christ's life is evident in our own lives. This quality is new to us.

Becoming what you look at

In 2 Corinthians, Paul teaches us that the more we look at Christ, the more we are changed into the same image. When we look at the living ascended Christ it is like learning who we really are in the new man. Therefore, Paul says it is like looking in a mirror where we see ourselves more clearly – the word "glass" is Old English for mirror:

> "But we all, with open face beholding as in a glass the glory of the Lord, are changed into the same image from glory to glory, *even* as by the Spirit of the Lord." (2 Corinthians 3:18)

We become what we look at. Paul pursued this transformation in his own life:

> "….but I follow after, if that I may apprehend that for which also I am apprehended of Christ Jesus" (Philippians 3:12).

The word "apprehend" here means to take hold. Today, we use this word in the sense of the police apprehending a suspect for a crime. The police will lay hold on that person and even handcuffing them for the purpose of arrest. Jesus Christ took hold of us so that he could give us everything he is. Now we are to take hold of these very things and make them our own through knowing the Christ in us by experience. This knowing in experience will grow us up in our new man. We grow up into Christ, into all the things that Christ is himself.

Therefore, we become living epistles:

> "*Forasmuch as ye are* manifestly declared to be the epistle of Christ ministered by us, written not with ink, but with the spirit of the living God; not in tables of stone, but in fleshy tables of the heart." (2 Corinthians 3:3)

We live the written Word, particularly that which is addressed to us in the letters of Paul. We are living epistles.

The knowledge of the secret

Let's take a further look at this word *"epignosis"* in relation to the Great Secret in the epistles. Paul prayed for us:

> "That the God of our Lord Jesus Christ, the Father of glory, may give unto you the spirit of wisdom and revelation in the knowledge [Gr. *"epignosis"*] of him" (Ephesians 1:17).

Paul's prayer was that we would come to know God experientially through the revelation and wisdom of the Great Secret being opened up to us.

In Colossians, Paul prayed that we would be filled with the knowledge of His will and increase in the knowledge of God:

> "For this cause we also, since the day we heard *it*, do not cease to pray for you, and to desire that ye might be filled with the knowledge [Gr. *"epignosis"*] of his will in all wisdom and spiritual understanding;
>
> That ye might walk worthy of the Lord unto all pleasing, being fruitful in every good work, and increasing in the knowledge [Gr. *"epignosis"*] of God". (Colossians 1:9-10)

These verses refer to us not only acquiring the knowledge of the Great Secret and but also being filled with it and thereafter holding it in all its wisdom and spiritual understanding. This is beautiful. This refers to the mature in Christ, those who are being perfected in him. These are Christians who increase in the true knowledge of God through living the Great Secret. Christ is manifest in their walks and lives through the multifaceted wisdom of God in the secret.

The phrase "in all wisdom and spiritual understanding" means that the knowledge of this secret is applied in real life. It's not just a theology or some religious practice, but rather is lived and applied in life. The nature of Christ is put forth and manifest in the way we live. Interestingly, rightly dividing the Word involves the correct application of a particular part of the Word of God to life's situations in the right way through spiritual understanding. It's not a misapplication of the Word.

> "That their hearts might be comforted, being knit together in love, and unto all riches of full assurance of understanding, to the acknowledgement [Gr. *"epignosis"*] of the mystery of God, and of the Father, and of Christ" (Colossians 2:2).

In the Greek texts, the word "acknowledgement" is *"epignosis"* meaning true knowledge gained by experience. It is Father's will that we all comprehend the Great Secret in all wisdom and spiritual understanding, and that our hearts are knit together in love in the Great Secret. He wants us all, as One Body, to be united in our hearts, to have the comfort and assurance that understanding the Great Secret brings and for all of us to go on to reach the true knowledge of God and the Great Secret.

In Philippians, Paul said those who are spiritually mature in Christ are to think like this. We are to lay hold on what God has made us to be in Christ.

> "Let us therefore, as many as be perfect, be thus minded: and if in anything ye be otherwise minded, God shall reveal even this unto you .... let us walk by the same rule, let us mind the same thing."(Philippians 3:15-16)

106

Part VII - The Great Secret of the One Body of Christ

Chapter 27: The truths of the One Body of Christ

Christ in you is only one part of the Great Secret. The second part is that all of us who have been born from above today are members of the One Body of Christ. In this section of the book, we shall begin to explore the wonderful truths concerning this part of the Great Secret.

The One Body of Christ, the Real Church

Despite the many different churches and groups within Christendom, God says that there is only one Church and that this one Church is the One Body of Christ:

> "*There is* one body…" (Ephesians 4:4)

There is only One Body of Christ not many bodies of Christ, despite man's efforts:

> "For as the body is one, and hath many members, and all the members of that one body, being many, are one body: so also *is* Christ." (1 Corinthians 12:12)

We are the Body of Christ which is the Church. All born again Christians belong to the One Body of Christ because we all have Christ in us.

> "… and gave him *to be* the head over all *things* to the church,
>
> Which is his body, the fulness of him that filleth all in all." (Ephesians 1:22-23)

So we are all the members of the One Body of Christ.

"Now ye are the body of Christ and members in particular."
(1 Corinthians 12:27)

A spiritual body

The Church in God's eyes is absolutely a spiritual entity and we should all grow to become faithful to what His Word declares about the Church. At the point where the emphasis on the physical overrides the spiritual truths of the One Body of Christ, there is grave error. The One Body of Christ is spiritual, not merely physical. The truths of the Church are spiritual and therefore must be spiritually discerned and understood. It has not been made with man's hands.

It's not a question of whether one church is true and all other denominations are false, as some may claim. Rather, the question to be posed to all denominations and groups is whether they are faithful to the truths of the household administration of the Great Secret in Christ or not. The true Church is the one that God has established – the true Church is the Great Secret of the One Body of Christ. The faithful church is any denomination or group that spiritually abides by the household administration of the Great Secret in Christ. All else is unfaithful, false and in error.

We know that there is an abundance of disregard to these truths in Christendom, yet the Word of God declares that He will destroy all who defile the Great Secret of the One Body of Christ:

"If any man defile the temple of God, him shall God destroy; for the temple of God is holy, which *temple* ye are."
(1 Corinthians 3:17)

How important and precious to God is the Great Secret that He will destroy any man who defiles it! God holds this Great Secret in high regard. Interestingly, we learned in an earlier chapter that if the Adversary had known the secret, he would not have crucified Jesus Christ. Therefore, from both God's and the Adversary's point of views, these truths convey to us the magnitude and the significance of the Great Secret. Both God and the Adversary know the greatness of this secret. It is often man who fails to see the significance of the secret. Yet, God has chosen to reveal it to us so that we would walk faithfully in it.

Entrance via the gift of holy spirit

You and I became members of the Body of Christ because we received the one spirit of Christ,

> "For by one spirit are we all baptised into one body, whether *we be* Jews or Gentiles, whether *we be* bond or free; and have been all made to drink into one spirit." (1 Corinthians 12:13)

We have all been made members of the One Body because God has given us the spirit of Christ. Within this one spirit, there is God's workmanship for He has created us in Christ. The workmanship is our new nature, our born again man. This is our true part in the Body of Christ. This is how we have been baptised into the One Body.

> "Therefore if any man *be* in Christ, *he is* a new creature: old things are passed away; behold all things are become new" (2 Corinthians 5:19).

That which is in the Body of Christ is the new man.

God set us in the One Body as it has pleased Him

Your position in the Body of Christ has been set by God. He has included you and no man can exclude you.

> "But now hath God set the members every one of them in the body, as it hath pleased him." (1 Corinthians 12:18)

Your place in the Body of Christ is God-made not man-made.

Jews and Gentiles

It was always known that the Gentile nations would be blessed with Israel. There are many scriptures declaring this in the Old Testament, but it was never conceived that the Gentiles would become part of the same body. Neither was it conceived that for both Israel and Gentiles that some of them would become the Body of Christ. This was a secret that God had hid in Himself.

> "That the Gentiles should be fellow-heirs, and of the same body, and partakers of his promise in Christ by the gospel" (Ephesians 3:6)

and,

> "And that he might reconcile both unto God in one body by the cross, having slain the enmity thereby" (Ephesians 2:16)

This One Body and this one calling had been kept secret in God. Interestingly, the Christ was to be Israel's bridegroom and Israel was to be the bride. Israel had always known that their redeemer would come as their bridegroom. They were to be the bride and their redeemer king was to be the bridegroom. But Israel never knew that some of them would be called out to become a member of Christ's Body. The truth of the One Body had been kept secret and hid in God until revealed to Paul as the household administration. Both Jews and Gentiles were now being called out to be part of the bridegroom.

Today, we are the Body of Christ, and Christ is still Israel's bridegroom. To understand this, we must spiritually discern what the Body of Christ is all about and how we are members of it.

Chapter 28: The significance of the One Body of Christ

The significance of the One Body of Christ to you and I has many aspects. But at this point I would like for us to consider just two aspects:

The first point to know: we are born again as the One New Man

Firstly, we are members of the Body of Christ because we have been born from above as a new man by way of the spirit of Christ. Because we have Christ in us we are thereby members of the Body of Christ. Furthermore, our new nature is the nature of Christ and of God. This is why Peter declares that we are partakers of the divine nature. So, in Ephesians, we learn that Christ, out of two (the Jews and the Gentiles), made one new man in himself.

> "Having abolished in his flesh the enmity, *even* the law of commandments *contained* in ordinances; for to make in himself of twain one new man, *so* making peace;
>
> And that he might reconcile both unto God in one body by the cross, having slain the enmity thereby;" (Ephesians 2:15-16)

Notice here that God declares that Jesus Christ made one new man and this making occurred in himself. It was exactly out of this "in himself" that the One Body of Christ was born.

The one new man is our born again man that was created in Christ. This is what we become, whether we were formerly Jews or Gentiles, it makes no difference. We all become the one new born again man in Christ. We actually become one new man in the One Body of Christ, with Christ being the Head and we being the members of that Body.

And because it is Christ in us, we all look like Christ in our new nature. From the outside looking in, the entire Body of Christ, because of spirit, looks like Christ. The new man is all Christ:

> "Where there is neither Greek nor Jew, circumcision nor uncircumcision, Barbarian, Scythian, bond *nor* free: but Christ *is* all, and in all." (Colossians 3:11)

Christ is not only in us, but also our new man is entirely Christ and nothing else. Take a look at the following verse in Ephesians which speaks of his Body and the members of it:

> "Which is his body, the fulness of him that filleth all in all." (Ephesians 1:23)

Not only is Christ in all, he is all in the new man. Also, in the new man, it is the fulness of Christ that fills all in all. Therefore, we were born again or born from above as the one new man in Christ. And yet, there is even more richness of the Great Secret for us to understand.

The second point to know: we are now to grow up into the Head

Our second point to consider is God declares it to be His will that we, as members of the Body of Christ, are all to grow up into the head. That is, even grow up into Christ himself who is the head of this spiritual One Body and he is the complete perfect man.

> "But speaking the truth in love, may grow up into him in all things, which is the head, *even* Christ:" (Ephesians 4:15)

The words "all things" refer to all that Christ is. Therefore, this salvation from our Father means that, in growing up into the head, we are to become all of what Christ is. We grow up into

Christ in all things. In other words, God has set us on a course to become the perfect man.

> "Till we all come in the unity of the faith, and [*in the unity*] of the knowledge of the Son of God, unto a perfect man, unto the measure of the stature of the fulness of Christ:"
> (Ephesians 4:13)

The word "unto" in the above verse is "*eis*" in the Greek which means that we arrive or attain to it; that is, we are to actually become what is being spoken of. We are talking about the perfect man, the Christ, the Son of God. Not only did Jesus Christ give his earthly life for us, he is also now giving us his heavenly life as the ascended perfect Son of the Father. We have certainly been given the power to become the sons of the living God.

Firstly, we received the spirit of Christ in us which is our born again or born from above new spirit man. At this point the Word says that we are simply babes, created perfect in Christ but not yet fully grown up into him. Then, God our Father begins the process of nurturing us to grow us up spiritually into the head of the One Body in all things. We will grow up to become all of what Jesus Christ is. This is the Great Secret and the wisdom of God. This is our great salvation.

> "Being confident of this very thing, that He which hath begun a good work in you will perform *it* until the day of Christ:"
> (Philippians 1:6)

The reason why the Father will continue this work only until the day of Christ, is that by that time Christ will have already gathered up all the members of the One Body of Christ and we shall have been made fully like him.

> "Beloved, now are we the sons of God, and it doth not yet appear what we shall be: but we know that, when he shall appear, we shall be like him; for we shall see him as he is.

And every man that hath this hope in him purifieth himself, even as he is pure." (1 John 3:2-3)

This is what the Bible declares as "the hope of his calling". Paul prayed that our hearts would be opened by God so that we may know the hope of this calling:

"The eyes of your understanding being enlightened; that ye may know what is the hope of his calling, and what the riches of the glory of his inheritance in the saints," (Ephesians 1:18)

Conclusion

Hence, the One Body of Christ is not physical but spiritual. God describes it as the one new man with Christ the Head. We have the perfect spirit in us and by that we are new babes, perfect in spirit but not yet fully grown into all the realities of the perfect man, the Son of God Jesus Christ.

Today, we think of the church as a physical building or a denominational organisation. We think of the Roman Catholic Church or the Baptist Church, or the Anglican Church and so on. Indeed, there are many churches. There are even numerous claims from some groups that they alone are the true church!! Surely, all of this appears foolish in light of God's perspective. The Body of Christ is spiritual and made up of people. It is not a man made organisation, neither is it physical since we know that the one new man is created in spirit.

The physical building of a church is no more than a physical place to meet in. Certainly, the members of the Body of Christ need a place to meet, but the focal point should always be what God has made us to be in Christ, that is One Body. We have seen in an earlier chapter that the administration or government of the household of God is to be the Great Secret. Yet it appears that man is guilty of replacing all this with something different, with something far less.

Therefore, the pertinent question is, are we faithful to God and His revealed Word regarding the administration of the Church in the Bible?

God made the One Body creating the one new man in Christ and thereby establishing the One Body of Christ which is the real church. This church exists in spirit not as a man-made organisation. Man's mind and even the mind of many Christians seem to be carnal and sold out to disobedience. Such a mind is in direct opposition to the Great Secret.

Man has been eager to build his version of the Church. But God says that He himself has placed every member in the One Body as it hath pleased Him, not as it hath pleased man. Yet man himself so often struggles to believe this and trust in God. However, we shall be faithful.

Chapter 29: The temple of God and the tabernacle of God

A difference

Before we delve further into the Great Secret of the One Body, we need to establish that there is a difference between the temple of God and the tabernacle of God. The difference is quite simple.

Collectively, all of God's sons in Christ make up the temple of God. However, individually we are each a tabernacle of God. It is important to be clear on this difference, so that the scriptures dealing with these truths can be properly understood. No end of confusion has been caused by getting these two points mixed up.

The temple of God

Paul challenged the believers in Corinth:

> "Know ye not that ye are the temple of God, and *that* the spirit of God dwelleth in you?
>
> If any man defile the temple of God, him shall God destroy; for the temple of God is holy, which *temple* ye are."
> (1 Corinthians 3:16-17).

The usages of the word "ye" in these verses are all plural and refer to all of God's sons in Christ. Collectively, we are the temple of the living God.

The tabernacle of God

However, individually, we are each a tabernacle of God.

> "For we know that if our earthly house of *this* tabernacle were dissolved, we have a building of God, an house not made with hands, eternal in the heavens." (2 Corinthians 5:1)

Our earthly house that Paul refers to is our physical bodies. Paul knew that it was God in Christ in our physical bodies. That is why he calls it "our earthly house of this tabernacle". A few verses before, Paul had declared that "we have this treasure in earthen vessels" (2 Corinthians 4:7).

Peter spoke of his physical body being a tabernacle, but that he would soon die and put off his physical body:

> "Yea, I think it meet, as long as I am in this tabernacle, to stir you up by putting *you* in remembrance;
>
> Knowing that shortly I must put off *this* my tabernacle, even as our Lord Jesus Christ hath shewed me.
>
> Moreover I will endeavour that ye may be able after my decease to have these things always in remembrance."
> (2 Peter 1:13-15)

Individually therefore, we are tabernacles for God, but collectively, we are the temple of God.

The Body of Christ grows into the temple

The more we grow up into Christ in all that he is, the more we grow as the temple of God:

> "In whom all the building fitly framed together groweth unto an holy temple in the Lord" (Ephesians 2:21)

and,

> "In whom ye also are builded together for an habitation of God through the spirit." (Ephesians 2:22)

The living temple is the One Body of the perfect man. This temple is built out of that part in us which is in the image of God. God's desire is to dwell in a living temple of believers in the collective part that is the new man, Christ in us the perfect man, the son of God. His sons, who are being changed into the image of His Son Jesus Christ, are the temple.

Conclusion

The Body of Christ is a spiritual house. In Old Testament times, there was a physical temple made of stone. In this Age of Grace that we live, the temple is made of people, or more accurately, it is made up of the new creation that is in all born again sons of God.

It is not difficult for God's sons to see spiritually. We walk by faith not by sight. We behold the temple as the one new man in Christ, which is our true identity, the true Church set up by the Father. In Ephesians 3:9, Paul laboured to make all men see the household administration of this One Body.

Chapter 30: *"Ekklesia"* - called out to the Great Secret in Christ

The real Church

Many people today wrongly understand the meaning of the word "Church" spoken of in the Epistles. They simply do not know what it is and it is not uncommon for the truth to be substituted with grave error. Hence, we see so many different divisions and every wind of the doctrines of men. However, in this chapter, I want for us to finally establish clearly what the Church is in reality. This means that we will need to disregard man's entire viewpoint and the worldly definition of the Church. Instead, we will adopt God's viewpoint and see the Church through spiritual eyes in order to have perfect understanding; and in so doing, we will be in "the obedience of faith" (Romans 16:25-26).

Ekklesia – the called out

The Greek word for church is *"ekklesia"*. This word does not really mean "church" at all at least in the way we think of the church today. Rather, in the Greek, this word literally means called out. Therefore, two questions arise: what are we called out from and more importantly, what are we called out to? The answer to these questions will help us understand what the true church really is.

Called out from and called out to

We are called out from the world to which we have become dead:

> "But God forbid that I should glory, save in the cross of our Lord Jesus, by whom the world is crucified unto me, and I unto the world." (Galatians 6:14)

We are called out from the world where we were formerly either a Jew or a Gentile to now become the one new man in Christ:

"..........for to make in himself of twain [*two*] one new man, *so* making peace

And that he might reconcile both unto God in one body..."
(Ephesians 2:15-16)

Remember, the Church is the Body of Christ. In his personal body, Jesus Christ made the one new man which is all Christ, or rather it is comprised of all things Christ. This one new man is the Church, the called out, the Body of Christ. In this one new man there is neither Jew nor Gentile. Even Paul counted all his Jewish status as excrement so that he could replace it with Christ:

"Yea doubtless, and I count all things *but* loss for the excellency of the knowledge of Christ Jesus my Lord: for whom I have suffered the loss of all things, and do count them *but* dung, that I may win Christ" (Philippians 3:8)

Today, we are no longer Jews or Gentiles. Rather we have become the one new man in the Body of Christ. We live by the faith of Jesus Christ and thereby grow up into the head of this One Body to become what Christ is, the perfect man.

"Till we all come in the unity of the faith, and [*the unity*] of the knowledge of the Son of God, unto a perfect man, unto the measure of the stature of the fulness of Christ.....

But speaking the truth in love, may grow up into him in all things, which is the head, *even* Christ"
(Ephesians 4:13 and 15).

We die to this world so that we may live the Christ in us, our new nature.

> "I am crucified with Christ: yet nevertheless I live; yet not I, but Christ lives in me: and the life which I now live in the flesh I live by the faith of the Son of God....." (Galatians 2:20)

In the Body of Christ we grow up into him in all things.

Other uses of the word *"ekklesia"* in the Bible

In fact, in the Bible the word *"ekklesia"* is not used exclusively for the Church. For example, in Acts 19 there was a large group of silversmiths who assembled together for a protest. They waged against Paul because they claimed that his teachings were causing people to discard their purchases of idol objects from which they made their living. The whole assembly ended up as a riot and in confusion. God refers to them as an *"ekklesia"*:

> "Some therefore cried one thing, and some another: for the assembly [*'ekklesia'*] was confused; and the more part knew not wherefore they were come together." (Acts 19:32)

This group of silversmiths was a church. In other words, they were called out for a common purpose – in this case it was for a protest against the Word of God!

Conclusion

The Greek word for "Church" used in the Bible really means to be called out for a purpose *(ekklesia)*. There has been major disobedience and apostasy in this area. Many Christians have sadly busied themselves with the physical and lost the real spiritual understanding and impact of these truths.

What we have just looked at in this chapter is God's explanation of what the Church is. It is surprisingly different to what many mean today when they speak of the Church. The worldly meaning of "Church" has changed from all recognition of what God originally intended. This worldly meaning has been passed down to us by tradition and not by truth.

We have been called out from something ugly and ungodly to embrace something that is godly and beautiful, that is the perfect new man created in Christ. We have not been called out to simply return to the ugliness and ungodliness of the world where we came from. That would be the Adversary's desire. Rather, when we walk in the original meaning of God's revelation of the Church, vistas of understanding open up to us with all of God's blessings in this Great Secret. Therefore, we will walk faithfully in this great revelation:

> "Brethren, be followers together of me, and mark them which walk so as ye have us for an ensample." (Philippians 3:17)

When God speaks of the Church, He means the called out ones. He means all those who have been called out to embrace the Great Secret in Christ. The next time someone asks you "Do you go to Church?" you can explain to them that you are the Church because you are a called out one to the Great Secret in Christ.

So, what have we been called out to? We have been called out to the faith of Jesus Christ, to the One Body of Christ, to the one new man. We have been called out to the fullness of the Great Secret of Christ in us and the one new man, the Body of Christ where Christ is all and in all.

Chapter 31: The Great Secret of the One New Man (Part One)

The one new man in Christ was a secret that God had kept hid in Himself.

One New Man – God's workmanship

The true Church is the Body of Christ which is one new man. To see the church spiritually as it truly is, we will see that the true Church looks like one new man which it is in Christ. He is the head and we, who have been born from above, are the members. It is God's will that every member grows up into the head, which means that we are to be conformed or fashioned into the image of Christ. This is the one new man that the Bible refers to. It was God who first created this new man in Christ:

"For we are his workmanship created in Christ Jesus..." (Ephesians 2:10)

Jesus Christ makes Jews and Gentiles one new man in himself

Once God had created the new man in Christ, it was now available for His Son Jesus Christ to make us all as one new man in himself:

"But now in Christ Jesus ye who sometimes were far off are made nigh by the blood of Christ......

.....for to make in himself of twain one new man, *so* making peace;

And that he might reconcile both unto God in one body by the cross, having slain the enmity thereby"
(Ephesians 2:13, 15b, 16).

"Christ is all and in all"

In the new man, Christ is all and in all. This means that Christ is in you as the new man and that everything in that new man is Christ.

> "And have put on the new *man*, which is renewed in knowledge after the image of him that created him:
>
> Where there is neither Greek nor Jew, circumcision, Barbarian, Scythian, bond *nor* free: but Christ *is* all, and in all." (Colossians 3:10-11)

These are the precious truths of the Great Secret. The new man is comprised of all things Christ. He is all things in the new man, and there is nothing in the new man that is not Christ.

> "Therefore if any man *be* in Christ, *he is* a new creature: old things are passed away; behold, all things are become new.
>
> And all things *are* of God, who hath reconciled us to himself by Jesus Christ..." (2 Corinthians 5:17-18)

This new creature is the new creation which is the new man. It is God's own workmanship. He worked to create this in Christ. Therefore, everything in the new man is of God. In other words, the all things of the new man are God's workmanship in Christ. That's why the new man is perfect. It was created by God Himself in his own image of righteousness and true holiness, which is Christ.

> "And that ye put on the new man, which after God is created in righteousness and true holiness." (Ephesians 4:24)

The old dies and the new is living

We die to our own selves and become alive in the perfect new man that God has created in Christ in us:

> "And *that* he died for all, that they which live should not henceforth live unto themselves, but unto him which died for them, and rose again. (2 Corinthians 5:15).

Living unto Christ is literally living and walking in the new man. Whilst on earth, Jesus Christ gave himself to die and rise again for the salvation of all mankind. Today, Jesus Christ is far above the heavens and through God's workmanship he now also imparts his life to us. It is his eternal life, which is righteous, holy and pure. He is the ascended living and victorious Christ. The life of Christ is the very nature and image of God Himself. All of this dwells in us.

So great is the salvation of our Father through Jesus Christ His Son. Jesus Christ made this one new man in himself. We are no longer Jews, Gentiles, or anything else for that matter. We are a new creation in Christ and all things new are of God. In Christ old things have passed away. We are the one new man in Christ. This is our appointed identity. The significance of the One Body of Christ is that we are all one new man in him. Both Jews and Gentiles become dead to themselves so as to become one new man in Christ. We are all to grow up into the head of this One Body.

One spirit with the Lord

The Great Secret is that we are one spirit with the Lord Jesus Christ.

> "But he that is joined to the Lord is one spirit.
> (1 Corinthians 6:17)

This one spirit is the one new man where Christ is all. Paul wrote to the Christians in Ephesus explaining this to them

> "For this cause shall a man leave his father and mother, and shall be joined unto his wife, and they two shall be one flesh.
>
> This is a [*the texts read 'the'*] great mystery: but I speak concerning Christ and the church." (Ephesians 5:31-32)

Being one spirit with the Lord Jesus Christ, who is the head, we die to ourselves so that we may become what Christ is. In the sense that a man leaves his parents to become one with his wife, we leave our own selves (our old nature) so that we may become the one new man in Christ. This is what the Bible means when it says that we are one spirit with the Lord Jesus Christ. Paul says that this is the Great Secret concerning Christ and the church.

Being joined with the Lord as one spirit, our way is to grow up into the head in all things. We are not just a part of the Body of Christ; in the spirit, we are what Christ is and we have been called by God who raised him from the dead to grow up into Christ in all things so that we actually become what he is and manifest what he is. This is dealt with later in more detail in chapters within Part IX entitled "The Great Secret and the Heart of Man". We do not live for Christ, we live Christ. Paul would say that it is Christ who lives in us and the life that we now live, we live by the faith of the Son of God who gave himself for us. It is because our appointed identity is Christ that we live unto him and lay hold on that for which he laid hold on us for. We so walk, that by holding the head which is Christ, we make these realities our own.

We grow into the perfect man, Christ Jesus

Paul spoke of us all arriving at the true experiential knowledge of the Son of God; that we all become the perfect man:

> "Till we all come in the unity of the faith, and of the knowledge of the Son of God, unto a perfect man, unto the measure of the stature of the fulness of Christ, unto a perfect man, unto the measure of the stature of the fulness of Christ" (Ephesians 4:13)

The above verse refers to us maturing after us knowing by experience the Son of God. The new man was created according to God's image. The new man has been born in all Christians through God's own work. It is what God has made Christ to be to us. It is not separate from us, but rather it is in us by way of the gift of holy spirit. But now we have to learn what it is all about. We have to grow up in our hearts to become what God has made us to be in Christ.

Put on the new

We are to put on the new man in our hearts:

> "And that ye put on the new man, which after God is created in true righteousness and holiness." (Ephesians 4:24)

The Great Secret is addressed to the new man

All the riches of the glory of the secret are addressed to the new man and are about the new man. All the promises in the epistles are addressed to the new man. It is the new man who can stand before God in true righteousness and holiness. It is the new man which has every spiritual blessing in Christ. In the new man, God's grace has wrought a work that only God could have achieved. He has made every Christian equal with Christ in our standing together as the one new man of the One Body. Such is the wisdom of our Father.

This one new man is all Christ and we have all been made into the one new man and are thus presented to God by Jesus Christ as One Body. Our heavenly Father has abounded towards us in all wisdom. The wisdom of this one new man had been appointed for our glory before the world began.

Chapter 32: The Great Secret of the One New Man (Part Two)

"Christ is all and in all"

In Christ all things of the new man are of God. The all things are Christ, who is of God. The Great Secret is that we were crucified with Christ in that we died to ourselves and to this world, but then God, in making us alive in Christ, blessed us with every spiritual blessing in the Christ in us.

Our new nature in Christ is both the place and the very part that we have in the One Body of Christ. These are God designed. Our entrance into the One Body of Christ is via receiving the same spirit of Christ:

> "For by one spirit are we all baptised into one body, whether *we be* Jews or Gentiles, whether *we be* bond or free; and have been all made to drink into one spirit." (1 Corinthians 12:13)

Our carnal fleshly nature has no place in the one new man and has no place in the One Body of Christ. Speaking of the new man in Colossians, Paul wrote

> "Where there is neither Greek nor Jew, circumcision nor uncircumcision, Barbarian, Scythian, bond *nor* free: but Christ *is* all, and in all." (Colossians 3:11)

The new man is all Christ and this is in every Christian. We are all one new man in the One Body of Christ. Our carnal nature is not in this one spiritual Body; rather, God has told us to count our old nature as dead. From God's perspective, it is dead anyway so in this we are aligning ourselves in obedience to God by embracing what He thinks. The carnal nature will serve only to defile the temple of God.

One new man – the temple – a spiritual house

Ephesians 2:21 speaks of this One Body as the temple of the living God.

> "In whom all the building fitly framed together groweth unto an holy temple in the Lord:
>
> In whom ye also are builded together for an habitation of God through the spirit." (Ephesians 2:21-22)

We have been called out to become the one new man in Christ. The Church of Jesus Christ is not a church at all, at least in the manner that we think of a church today. Rather, the Bible says that it is a spiritual house, which is not fully available to the human eye. It must be spiritually discerned. It is the One Body of Christ and each of us is growing into a holy spiritual temple for the Almighty God Himself to dwell. We are all growing up into the new man and we are putting on the new man in our hearts to become what Christ has laid hold on us for.

> "Lie not one to another, seeing that ye have put off the old man with his deeds;
>
> And have put on the new *man*, which is renewed in knowledge after the image of him that created him" (Colossians 3:9-10)

We are one spirit with the Lord Jesus Christ.

> "But he that is joined unto the Lord is one spirit." (1 Corinthians 6:17)

We are no longer simply our old selves. We have been brought by God to the new man and we are now growing up into it and thereby growing as a holy spiritual temple for God Himself to dwell in us.

> "I am [*was*] crucified with Christ: nevertheless I live; yet not I, but Christ liveth in me: and the life which I now live in the flesh, I live by the faith of the Son of God, who loved me and gave himself for me." (Galatians 2:20)

The Church of Jesus Christ is a people called out from the Jews and Gentiles to be a new nation, a new people or more accurately to become the one new man in Christ. That new man is Christ who is the Son of God, the perfect man. This is the true knowledge of the Son of God. This is the Great Secret that God had kept hid in Himself until He revealed it to the Apostle Paul.

In comprehending the Great Secret, you have to be sold out and totally convinced that God's work in you is to fashion you into Christ, the perfect man according to the image of God. You died with Christ and you are now free so believe that God will nurture you and grow you up into the new man. This new man is all Christ and this is in you.

We are one new man in Christ

In the Bible, God classifies people into three groups: Jews, Gentiles and those called out to become the one new man in Christ to make up the One Body of Christ.

> "Give none offence, neither to the Jews, nor to the Gentiles, nor to the church of God" (1 Corinthians 10:32)

Man will belong to one of these three groups.

It is interesting that strictly speaking today, according to the Word of God, there can be no such thing as Jews for Jesus. This is because both Jews and Gentiles who accept Jesus Christ die to themselves to become the one new man in the Body of Christ. Paul was a Hebrew of Hebrews yet he counted all his Hebrew status as dung, excrement, so that he could win Christ, so that he could become the one new man in Christ.

> "Circumcised the eighth day, of the stock of Israel, *of* the tribe of Benjamin, an Hebrew of the Hebrews; as touching the law, a Pharisee;
>
> Concerning zeal, persecuting the church; touching the righteousness which is in the law, blameless.
>
> But what things were gain to me, those I counted loss for Christ.
>
> Yea doubtless, and I count all things *but* loss for the excellency of the knowledge of Christ Jesus my Lord; for whom I have suffered the loss of all things, and do count them *but* dung, that I may win Christ" (Philippians 3:5-8).

Jews cease to be Jews when they become members of the Body of Christ. Likewise Gentiles cease to be Gentiles when they become members of the Body of Christ. If we hold on to our past old man, then there is no room in our hearts for Christ. Paul said that because of Christ, the whole world had been crucified to him and he had been crucified to the world. Herein is our true identity. We are neither Jews, nor Gentiles; we are not of this world: rather, we are the one new man belonging to the One Body of Christ.

> "But God forbid that I should glory, save in the cross of our Lord Jesus Christ, by whom the world is crucified unto me, and I unto the world.
>
> For in Christ Jesus neither circumcision availeth anything, nor uncircumcision, but a new creature.

And as many as walk according to this rule, peace *be* on them and mercy, and upon the Israel of God." (Galatians 6:14-16)

The Great Secret is more than just being Christ like

The Great Secret is that God, through Christ, is making a new nation of people who will grow up into the head of the One Body, to become what Christ is. We will all grow up into Christ. This is not being Christ like; it is much stronger and surer than that; we are becoming exactly what Christ is. We have died to ourselves so that we can become new. We become the one new man of the One Body of Christ where Christ is not only in all but he is all. So in truth, we are growing up into him, which is even closer than just becoming like him. We will not be Jews. We will not be Gentiles. We are members of Christ, the one new man. In the Body of Christ, we were made one new man where all things are new and are not of the flesh but are spiritual and of God.

"Therefore, if any man *be* in Christ, *he is* a new creature: old things are passed away; behold, all things are become new.

And all things *are* of God, who hath reconciled us to himself by Jesus Christ...." (2 Corinthians 5:17-18)

The new man is created by God from spirit and is new in quality. God created the new man according to His own image. Ephesians 2:10 says that the new man was created in Christ. This new man is perfect and is all Christ. We are truly sons of God. Jesus Christ is the firstborn of many.

The Body of Christ is truly the Church of the one new man. In other words, we have been called out to the one new man which is all Christ. Seeing the Church as the one new man in Christ is God's perspective as revealed in His Word. This is the Great Secret of Christ and the Church.

We become members of the Body of Christ by receiving the gift of spirit which is the spirit of Christ. This is the new man and this is holy spirit.

Chapter 33: The preaching of the Cross and the Great Secret (Part Two)

There are many riches that Jesus Christ accomplished for us through his cross.

Reconciled in One Body

Through the cross, we were reconciled to God:

> "And having made peace through the blood of the cross, by him to reconcile all things unto himself; by him, *I say*, whether *they be* things in earth, or things in heaven.
>
> And you, that were sometime alienated and enemies in *your* mind by wicked works, yet now hath he reconciled
>
> In the body of his flesh through death…...."
> (Colossians 1:20-22)

The living way

Not only did Jesus Christ reconcile us to God in One Body, but through his cross he opened up the living way to the Father. When he died, the veil that separated the holy of holies from the rest of the physical temple in Jerusalem was split in two. This was a sign from God that the way to him was now open:

> "Having therefore, brethren, boldness to enter into the holiest by the blood of Jesus,
>
> By a new and living way, which he hath consecrated for us, through the veil, that is to say his flesh" (Hebrews 10:19-20)

This living way was accomplished by the cross.

The making of the one new man in the One Body of Christ

The Father created the one new man in Christ:

> "For we are his workmanship, created in Christ Jesus unto good works…" (Ephesians 2:10)

Afterwards, Jesus Christ would make both Jews and Gentiles into this one new man in himself. Jesus Christ did this by his cross:

> "Having abolished in his flesh the enmity, *even* the law of commandments *contained* in ordinances; for to make in himself of twain one new man, *so* making peace;
>
> And that he might reconcile both unto God in one body by the cross, having slain the enmity thereby" (Ephesians 2:15-16).

Through the cross, Jesus Christ made the One Body of Christ which is the temple of God. This One Body is one of the two precepts of the Great Secret.

To present you holy and unblameable and unreproveable in his sight

Through the blood of the cross of Jesus Christ, we are reconciled to God. We will also be presented holy, unblameable and unreproveable:

> "And having made peace through the blood of the cross, by him to reconcile all things unto himself; by him, *I say*, whether *they be* things in earth, or things in heaven.
>
> And you, that were sometime alienated and enemies in *your* mind by wicked works, yet now hath he reconciled
>
> In the body of his flesh through death, to present you holy and unblameable and unreproveable in his sight."
> (Colossians 1:20-22)

Jesus Christ gave himself for the called out ones so that he could present us to himself as perfect in Christ:

"Husbands, love your wives, even as Christ also loved the church, and gave himself for it;

That he might sanctify and cleanse it with the washing of water by the word,

That he might present it to himself a glorious church, not having spot, or wrinkle, or any such thing; but that it should be holy and without blemish." (Ephesians 5:25-27)

In verse 32, Paul goes on to say that "This is the Great Mystery (Secret): but I speak concerning Christ and the church." Jesus Christ's intention is that through his cross we would be holy and without any blemish and perfected in him:

"According as he hath chosen us in him before the foundation of the world, that we should be holy and without blame before him in love" (Ephesians 1:4)

Abolished the Law

By his cross, Jesus Christ abolished the law so that we could live in the grace and in the love of God as the sons of the Father:

"Having abolished in his flesh the enmity, *even* the law of commandments *contained* in ordinances; for to make in himself of twain one new man, *so* making peace" (Ephesians 2:15).

He both fulfilled the law and then abolished the law when he made us into sons as the one new man.

He blotted out the law and nailed it to his cross:

"Blotting out the handwriting of ordinances that was against us, which was contrary to us, and took it out of the way, nailing it to his cross" (Colossians 2:14).

We now have peace with God. We have been reconciled to Him in the One Body. We are now in the living way and have boldness to enter into the holiest of all. We are perfect in Christ and his desire is to present us glorious, without blemish, holy, and unreproveable in love. Jesus Christ abolished the law that was contrary to us. He did all this by the cross.

Chapter 34: In the Great Secret not all have the same office

Two wonderful truths

In this chapter, we shall see that there are another two wonderful truths about the One Body of Christ that we need to firmly establish in our hearts. Firstly, our Father has set every member of the Body of Christ as it has pleased Him, and secondly, not all members have the same office or function in the Church. In this chapter, we shall explore these two truths.

It is God who has put you in your position in the Body of Christ:

> "But now hath God set the members every one of them in the body as it hath pleased him." (1 Corinthians 12:18)

God has set us all in the Body of Christ as it has pleased him. The word "set" is "*tithemi*" in the Greek which means to put in place and thereby ordain or appoint. Every Christian has been placed by God in a special position in the Body of Christ. Your place has God's stamp of approval and authority on it so don't let anyone belittle your place in the One Body. You should believe that your position is special because it is God appointed. It is God's standard. When referring to your place in the Body of Christ, this really means the role which God has appointed you to fulfill. Your place is not a dead seat but a living function. Interestingly, the more of the Word we understand, the more we will understand our particular position in the One Body.

All members have not the same office

Just like our physical bodies where we have hands, legs, and feet etc which all perform different functions, so too in the Body of Christ there are different members performing different functions to bless God's people. Paul uses the example of a physical human body to show how in the Body of Christ we are all different members holding different offices:

"For as we have many members in one body, and all members have not the same office:

So we, *being* many, are one body in Christ, and every one members one of another." (Romans 12:4-5)

All members have not the same office. As members, we may all have different offices or functions in the Body but all of the different functions are needed.

Gifts of grace

All born again Christians are members of the One Body and we have all received gift(s) of grace from God to bless the Church. Some have received grace to be a gift ministry to the Church such as apostles, prophets, teachers and pastors and evangelists. Others have received different gifts of grace which are not ministries but are extended ways to bless the Body of Christ such as exhorting their brothers and sisters in Christ, or showing great mercy with cheerfulness, or helps and so on. Paul explains this in the Epistle to the Romans:

"Having then gifts ["*charisma*"] differing according to the grace that is given to us, whether prophecy, *let us prophesy* according to the proportion of faith;

Or ministry, *let us wait on our ministering*: or he that teacheth, on teaching;

Or he that exhorteth, on exhortation: he that giveth, *let him do it* with simplicity; he that ruleth, with diligence; he that sheweth mercy with cheerfulness.

Let love be without dissimulation." (Romans 12:6-9)

All of these works are examples of gifts of grace (*"charisma"*) and are ordained by God; they have His stamp of approval and authority. We all have something from God to contribute to the Body of Christ.

Each work is special because it is from God and each function is needed for the spiritual health and growth of the Body of Christ. The more you grow in the Word of God, the more you will discover about your own place in the One Body of Christ and the *"charisma"* that are yours from God to bless the Church.

These gifts of grace are related to the *"tithemi"* act of our Father. Firstly, He gave us all spirit thereby making us all members of the Body of Christ. By one spirit we have all been baptized into the One Body of Christ. He then set us all in the Body of Christ in the particular positions or functions chosen by Him. He did this by gifts of grace (*"charisma"*) which determine our individual office. The head of the One Body, Jesus Christ, functions in all of these offices today. However, no member of the Body of Christ, other than the Head, has yet fully grown into all these abilities. Nevertheless, we all have these abilities or potential within us because we have Christ in us. All of the potential resides in Christ, who is in us. However, the truth is that we are all growing up into him and no one has yet been fully perfected or fully grown up into him. Nevertheless, the ability to do all of these things is resident in the spirit of Christ which is in us. Therefore, we are all in the process of growing up into him in all things. One day we will, after the Gathering Together, be fully perfected and fully grown up into him.

God's order and the "after that"

"And God hath set some in the church, first apostles,
secondarily prophets, thirdly teachers, after that miracles, then
gifts of healings, helps, governments, diversities of tongues."
(1 Corinthians 12:28)

Notice here God's order and how He set the various priorities: firstly apostles, who bring the new light of the Great Secret to God's people; then secondarily prophets who bring God's people back in the way of the Lord and back to His Word regarding the Great Secret; then thirdly teachers of the Word, who make plain God's will regarding the Great Secret to His people. Then God uses this stark phrase "after that". After appointing apostles, prophets, and teachers, He ordains workers of miracles and the gifts of healings. Interestingly, some Christians behave as if miracles and healings are the primary issue for Christianity, but God places them in His perspective. Then, after all these there are helps and those who give guidance, and then diversities of tongues.

The best gifts and the more excellent way

There is a statement in Corinthians that many have wrested to their own ruin:

"But covet earnestly the best gifts...." (1 Corinthians 12:31a)

The word "best" here should be translated "greater" and this refers to that which is required to build up the church and more particularly it refers to exactly what is required to fulfill a need. The word "gifts" here is "*charisma*" which means gifts of grace.

"For I long to see you, that I may impart unto you some
spiritual gift, to the end ye may be established"
(Romans 1:11).

The particular need may be an apostle or it may be gifts of healings or it may be spiritual guidance or helps. The immediate goal is that the believers may be led towards being established in the Great Secret (see also Romans 16:25-26), but the bigger goal is that after being established, the believers who had received ministering would be able with the minister to enjoy the comfort of the mutual believing of both.

> "That is, that I may comforted together with you by the mutual faith both of you and me." (Romans 1:12)

and,

> "That their hearts might be comforted, being knit together in love, and unto all riches of the full assurance of understanding, to the acknowledgment of the mystery, of God, and of the Father, and of Christ." (Colossians 2:2)

Is your church or fellowship group knit together in love and in living the Great Secret together, fully assured and enjoying the riches of all this? The goal for every fellowship or church is towards the Great Secret and all its benefits. However, there is an even more excellent way than pursuing the greater gifts of grace.

> "But covet earnestly the best [*greater*] gifts: and yet shew I unto you a more excellent way." (1 Corinthians 12:31)

The more excellent way is love because love is the end of the Word:

> "Now the end of the commandment is charity [*love of God*] out of a pure heart, and *of* a good conscience, and *of* faith unfeigned" (1Timothy 1:5).

The greater in 1 Corinthians Chapter 14

Here we move from gifts of grace to the correct usage of the manifestations of holy spirit in the church. The focus of this chapter is the edification or the building up of the members of the Body of Christ, and this is referred to as being a "greater" act.

> "…for greater *is* he that prophesieth than he that speaketh with tongues, except he interpret, that the church may receive edifying." (1 Corinthians 14:5b)

The building up of the Body of Christ refers to the members growing up into Christ the head. After showing the more excellent way of love in Chapter 13, Paul again picks up the theme of best or greater. The end of Chapter 12 speaks of the greater gifts; whilst Chapter 14 uses a figure of speech where the person spoken of refers to the work. It is said that greater is he (i.e. the work) who builds up the Body of Christ rather than just building up oneself.

The sum of all this is that God has placed us in the Body of Christ. The place refers to both the new man (spirit) and that particular function or office which is a service to the One Body of Christ. This service is comprised of gifts of God's grace. The best is greater in so far as it supplies what is needed towards presenting every person perfect in the Great Secret of Christ.

The renewed mind walk in Romans 12

The teaching of Romans chapter 12 is very illuminating. Romans 12:1-2 refers to us growing up into Christ and being transformed into him.

> "I beseech you therefore, brethren, by the mercies of God, that ye present your bodies a living sacrifice, holy, acceptable unto God, *which is* your reasonable service.
>
> And be not conformed to this world: but be ye transformed by the renewing of your mind, that ye may prove what *is* that good, and acceptable, and perfect, will of God."
> (Romans 12:1-2)

When we grow up into the head, we can do the will of God. The next section goes on to exhort every Christian not to think more highly than he ought to think just because we have received a certain gift of grace from God. We are reminded that there are many members in the One Body and that not every member has the same office. Not all have the same gifts of grace.

"For I say, through the grace given unto me, to every man that is among you, not to think *of himself* more highly than he ought to think; but to think soberly, according as God hath dealt to every man the measure of faith.

For as we have many members in one body, and all members have not the same office:

So we, being many, are one body in Christ, and every one members one of another." (Romans 12:3-5)

We are members of one another because in God's eyes we are all members of the One Body. The truth is that whatever we have, it has been given to us by God. We have been given it by grace; that is, we didn't merit it by own selves but rather it was given to us through God's own favour. It is definitely not something with which to elevate ourselves but rather to serve with; and that's the point. That is the humility that Paul is referring to here. In Ephesians 4:2, we are encouraged to walk "with all lowliness and meekness". The greatest among us is also the greatest servant; the greatest among us is not the person who has elevated himself.

"Having then gifts differing according to the grace that is given to us, whether prophecy, *let us prophesy* according to the proportion of faith;

Or ministry, *let us wait* on *our* ministering: or he that teacheth, on teaching;

146

Or he that exhorteth, on exhortation: he that giveth, *let him do it* with simplicity; he that ruleth, with diligence; he that sheweth mercy, with cheerfulness.

Let love be without dissimulation. Abhor that which is evil; cleave to that which is good." (Romans 12:6-9)

In Romans 12:6-8, we are reminded that not all members have the same gifts of grace. We are exhorted to get busy with whatever work God has appointed us to do. In Romans 12:9, we are reminded to let love be without hypocrisy. This love without hypocrisy is further opened up in the next verses. In honour, we are to prefer others in the Body of Christ rather than elevating our own gifts of grace and work merely to elevate ourselves. In other words, we are to esteem others in the Body of Christ more highly than ourselves. Philippians 2:3 says that "Let nothing be done through strife or vainglory; but in lowliness of mind let each esteem other better than themselves". We find the same here in the context of service:

"*Be* kindly affectioned one to another with brotherly love; in honour preferring one another;

Not slothful in business [*diligence*]; fervent in spirit; serving the Lord.......

Distributing to the necessity of the saints...."
(Romans 12:10-13)

How beautiful is God's instruction. There is no room for anything that amounts to glorying in the flesh. Rather, with affection as brothers we are to honour others in the One Body rather than ourselves, then in diligence and in being spiritually aglow with the Christ in us, we are to serve one another with whatever gifts of grace that we have.

147

The renewed mind walk in 1 Corinthians 12

The teaching in 1 Corinthians chapter 12 is complementary to Romans chapter 12. They go hand in hand. The Epistle to the Romans records the doctrine which is foundational to the fuller revelation of the Great Secret which is unfolded in Ephesians. However, Corinthians reproves those who are not walking according to the doctrine of Romans. Both sections in Romans and Corinthians relate to our walk in light of the One Body of Christ.

1 Corinthians 12:11 speaks of dividing the manifestations of holy spirit to every man severally as he wills because it is Christ in us.

"But all these worketh that one and selfsame spirit, dividing to every man severally as he will".

The next two verses highlight that just like your physical body has many parts (hands, legs, feet, eyes, ears etc) which are all part of your physical body, so are the members of the One Body of Christ. All born again believers are members of the One Body of Christ.

"For as the body is one, and hath many members, and all the members of that one body, being many, are one body: so also *is* Christ.

For by one spirit are we all baptized into one body, whether *we be* Jews or Gentiles, whether *we be* bond or free; and have been all made to drink into one spirit."
(1 Corinthians 12:12-13)

Paul then reaches the point to declare:

For the body [*of Christ*] is not one member, but many."
(1 Corinthians 12:14)

148

The Body of Christ is made up of different members and not simply one member. We are all encouraged to see this and walk accordingly. In the following verses the Word of God draws on a ridiculous and humorous conversation between the physical body parts of a person to show how we are all members of the spiritual One Body of Christ.

"If the foot shall say, Because I am not the hand, I am not of the body; is it therefore not of the body?

And if the ear shall say, Because I am not the eye, I am not of the body; is it therefore not of the body?

If the whole body *were* an eye, where *were* the hearing? If the whole *were* hearing, where *were* the smelling?"
(1 Corinthians 12:15-17)

Verse 17 asks the question if the whole body were an eye, then where would hearing have its place? No single office in the Body of Christ is the whole picture, neither does any exist by itself. From God's perspective, all parts need to be viewed as a whole.

In these verses, the physical body parts are mentioned to illustrate the spiritual parts of the Body of Christ. The Word of God teaches us that we are the members of Christ on two grounds. Firstly, we have the spirit of Christ in us, the new man which is all Christ. Secondly, when we walk in that new nature in service to others, we grow up into all of what that new nature is, which is the head, Christ. Our walking and growing relates to the different functions or offices in the Body of Christ. Interestingly, as we have seen earlier in this chapter, it is God who has set all the members in their particular office as it has pleased Him.

"But now hath God set the members every one of them in the body, as it hath pleased Him.

149

And if they were all one member, where *were* the body?"
(1 Corinthians 12:18-19)

God has placed us all in the Body of Christ and He has set all the members in their particular office as it has pleased Him. In other words, by grace God has given you an office or function in the Body of Christ as it has pleased Him. Therefore, the more we grow in the Word of God, the more we will come to understand our special function.

1 Corinthians 12:19 tells us that if the Body of Christ is all about one gift of grace, then where is the Body? In other words, what about the other members and functions? They are just as important as explained in 1 Corinthians 12:20-24.

"But now *are they* many members, yet but one body.

And the eye cannot say unto the hand, I have no need of thee: nor again the head to the feet, I have no need of you.

Nay, much more those members of the body, which seem to be more feeble, are necessary:

And those *members* of the body, which we think to be less honourable, upon these we bestow more abundant honour; and our uncomely *parts* have more abundant comeliness.

For our comely *parts* have no need: but God hath tempered the body together, having given more abundant honour to that *part* which lacked" (1 Corinthians 12:20-24)

The Word of God tells us that God has tempered the One Body of Christ so that the less comely parts have more abundant honour. Clearly, Paul had to reprove some believers in Corinth because they had not tempered their understanding to walk in accordance with the Great Secret. Rather, they had elevated both themselves and others by not adhering to the truth of the One Body and how God had established it in the Great Secret.

God's heart for the Body of Christ is at the heart of the Great Secret:

> "That there should no schism in the body, but *that* the members should have the same care one for another.
>
> And whether one member suffer, all the members suffer with it; or one member be honoured, all the members rejoice with it." (1 Corinthians 12:25-26)

This is the oneness that God has set. Isn't that beautiful?

Recent years

In recent years there has been a tendency for some Christians to elevate the words that Jesus Christ spoke to the twelve Apostles:

> "Heal the sick, cleanse the lepers, raise the dead, cast out devils: freely ye have received, freely give." (Matthew 10:8)

Some people wrongly think that this is the blueprint for the Great Secret and that every Christian should be doing these works today. However, the ability and power to do these works is certainly in every Christian because we all have Christ in us; but, there is sometimes an immature tendency to glorify these works as the mainstay of Christianity. However, when we go to the Word of God, a different picture emerges. Jesus Christ commanded the twelve Apostles not go to the Gentiles but to the lost sheep of the house of Israel. This is significant. They were not offering the gospel of the Grace of God in the Great Secret but gospel of the king and the kingdom of heaven to Israel:

"These twelve Jesus sent forth, and commanded them saying, Go not into the way of the Gentiles, and into *any* city of the Samaritans enter ye not:

But go rather to the lost sheep of the house of Israel.

And as ye go, preach, saying, The kingdom of heaven is at hand.

Heal the sick, cleanse the lepers, raise the dead, cast out devils: freely ye have received, freely give." (Matthew 10:5-8)

In this Age of Grace that we live, our task is not to ignore the Gentiles for we were once Gentiles ourselves. Our gospel is not the gospel of the kingdom of heaven but rather it is the gospel of the grace of God in the Great Secret. This is the household administration and there is now an entirely different focus. We are now part of the One Body of Christ and we are now to grow up into the Head. We do not preach the kingdom of heaven but we preach "Jesus Christ according to the revelation of the mystery, which was kept secret since the world began ..... for the obedience of faith" (Romans 16:25 and 26). Therefore, we need to mature to understand this difference.

Conclusion

In the Great Secret not all have the same office or function. God has set some in the church as apostles, prophets and teachers; after that, miracles, then gifts of healings, helps, governments, diversities of tongues. Moreover, God has placed us in our individual office and we are all to grow up into Christ in all things. We are members one of another in the One Body of Christ.

Part VIII - The Gospel of the Glory of Our Lord Jesus Christ

Chapter 35: The gospel of the glory of Our Lord Jesus Christ

Gospels

The word "gospel" means good news. There are many gospels in the Bible such as the Gospel of God, the Gospel of the Kingdom of Heaven, The Gospel of the Kingdom of God, the Gospel of the Grace of God, and the Eternal Gospel and more. These are all separate and distinct within their own right, and have different meanings. However, the Gospel of the Glory of Our Lord Jesus Christ is a special gospel that relates to the Great Secret that was given to Paul.

"But if our gospel be hid, it is hid to them that are lost:

In whom the god of this world hath blinded the minds of them which believe not, lest the light of the glorious gospel of Christ, who is the image of God, should shine unto them." (2 Corinthians 4:3-4).

The words "glorious gospel of Christ" are literally the "gospel of the glory of Christ". Father declares that we are to have the light of this gospel shining both to us and in us.

"For God, who commanded the light to shine out of darkness, hath shined in our hearts, to *give* the light of the knowledge of the glory of God in the face of Jesus Christ.

But we have this treasure in earthen vessels, that the excellency of the power may be of God and not of us." (2 Corinthians 4:6-7)

In Christ we are shown the very glory of God. The new man is glorious because he is created in the glory of God. By our

Father's undeserved kindness (grace), we are brought into the very centre of this gospel. In other words, we have been given a major role in it. In this chapter we will explore our part in the gospel of the glory of our Lord Jesus Christ.

"Doxa"

The Greek word for glory is *"doxa"*. It means light, shining, brightness, majesty, honour, supreme honour, excellence. The power of God has all these qualities. *"Doxa"* in the context of the Gospel of the Glory of our Lord Jesus Christ refers to the royal dignity of the king. We have received the spirit of Christ (gift of holy spirit) to dwell in us continuously. Everything in that spirit is glorious. And God's future work in us will also be glorious. Let us take a look at our part in this gospel.

The Great Secret appointed for our glory

God declares that He appointed the Great Secret for our glory. The Great Secret that He had kept hidden in Himself is for our glory. He wants to glorify you and I with this Great Secret:

> "But we speak the wisdom of God in a mystery, *even* the hidden *wisdom* which God ordained before the world unto our glory" (1 Corinthians 2:7).

It is for our glory. God's intention is to bring us into the very heart of the Gospel of the Glory of Our Lord Jesus Christ. God will show us how He has given us a central role in this gospel. He has declared that today, we can begin to walk with this glory in us.

Glory now and glory future

Colossians 1:27 refers to this glory both in terms of what our Father has provided for us now and what He will provide for us in the future:

> "To whom God would make known what *is* the riches of the glory of this mystery among the Gentiles, which is Christ in you the hope of glory" (Colossians 1:27)

There is glory available right now and there is more glory to come in the future. Today, God is making known to us what are the riches of the glory of this secret of Christ in us. And in the same verse, He shows us that we also have the hope of Christ's future glory.

In our language today, the word "hope" has a ring of uncertainty about it. It is often used of something that might or might not happen. We hear phrases like "I hope we win the match" and "I hope it doesn't rain" and "I hope we get there on time" and so on. However, in the times when the Bible was written, the word hope would refer to a certainty that would definitely happen but was simply future. The phrase "hope of glory" refers to the future glory of Christ that will one day belong to us also.

So, the gospel of the glory of our Lord Jesus Christ provides us with glory today and further glory for us in the future.

> "Whereunto he called you by our gospel, to the obtaining of the glory of our Lord Jesus Christ." (2 Thessalonians 2:14)

God's Word declares that we have been called through the gospel of the Great Secret to obtain the glory of our Lord Jesus Christ. This is a very powerful statement as it relates to both the glory that Jesus Christ has been given today by the Father as well as his future glory as the King of Kings and Lord of Lords. We have been called to obtain both glories. Today, we have already been glorified with the risen Christ in us:

> "For whom he did foreknow, he also did predestinate *to be* conformed to the image of his Son, that he might be the firstborn among many brethren.

> Moreover whom he did predestinate, them he also called: and whom he called, them he also justified: and whom he justified, them he also glorified." (Romans 8:29-30)

Jesus Christ ascended to the Father and has been glorified and is now seated at the right hand of God. As he is today, so are we in this world (1 John 4:17). This is because the ascended glorious Christ lives in us today. This is what Paul was referring to when he said that we have already been glorified. Yet, as we have seen, there is even more glory to come:

> "..... that we may also be glorified together.

> For I reckon that the sufferings of this present time *are* not worthy *to be compared* with the glory which shall be revealed in us." (Romans 8:17-18)

Changed into his glory today

God is changing the faithful today into the same image of Christ from one glory to another glory.

> "But we all, with open face beholding as in a glass the glory of the Lord, are changed into the same image from glory to glory, *even* as by the Spirit of the Lord." (2 Corinthians 3:18)

The phrase "from glory to glory" refers to the truth that every aspect of Jesus Christ is glorious. When we are being changed into different aspects of Christ, we are actually being changed from one glorious aspect of Christ to another glorious aspect as we grow up into him. What a wonderful truth. Every change that our Father works in us is glorious. Jesus Christ has already been glorified. As the world goes from corruption to corruption, we are different because we are being changed into him, from one glory to another glory. Ephesians 4:15 tells us that we are to grow up into Christ in all things. Every "thing" in Christ is glorious and in the each "thing" of Christ we grow up into, it is God who is transforming us from glory to glory.

Moses

After receiving the Law from God, Moses' countenance was so bright that the Israelites could not look at him directly. The face of Moses shone with a brightness and glory that they had never seen before. Moses had drawn near to God. But how much brighter are we to whom God has appointed the Great Secret for our glory. We have God in Christ dwelling in us. Today, God's sons are being patterned to Christ and the greatest glory of all is for us. Jesus Christ himself is the brightness of God's glory and Christ is in us.

"Who being the brightness of *his* glory, and the express image of his person" (Hebrews 1:3).

Today, we have the brightness of His glory being manifest in us. This shining appears in our hearts when our minds are made new and then the Father reveals His glory to us through the Christ in us. Today we are growing up into the head of the One Body in all things, even into Christ. We are being fashioned according to the image of Christ who is the very image of God's person. This is in us, today and we now have something greater than Moses. We have the glorious Christ born within us.

"….. Christ in you the hope of glory" (Colossians 1:27)

Chapter 36: The riches of the glory of the Great Secret (present)

Made rich in Christ

We have seen in an earlier chapter how God wants us to come to know the Great Secret in all of its depth. That said, His desire is to specifically make known today what are the riches of the glory of this secret. In Colossians 1:27, God had commanded Paul to make known what are the riches of the glory of this mystery. Knowing these riches is an essential part of comprehending the length, breadth, depth and height of the Great Secret.

> "To whom God would make known what *is* the riches of the glory of this mystery among the Gentiles, which is Christ in you the hope of glory" (Colossians 1:27)

Some of these riches are for the future, and some are for the immediate present time, right now. There is glory in us today because we have Christ in us. In this chapter we are going to look at some of the riches of having Christ in us.

Firstly, the Word of God declares that we have been made rich:

> "For ye know the grace of our Lord Jesus Christ, that, though he was rich, yet for your sakes he become poor, that ye through his poverty might be rich." (2 Corinthians 8:9).

Jesus Christ died so that he could make us rich. The riches referred to here are the riches of having Christ in us. When we look into the Word, we see how much God has enriched us. God is happy that He has blessed us with every spiritual blessing that is available in Christ. We too should be happy when we realise these truths:

"Blessed *be* the God and Father of our Lord Jesus Christ, who hath blessed us with all [*every*] spiritual blessings in heavenly *places* in Christ" (Ephesians 1:3).

The every spiritual blessing refers to how in Christ we are given all that Christ has and more significantly, all that he is. We even grow up into what he is in all things. Now that is rich! Yet, over the years how far below par we have lived: how much we have allowed the Adversary to talk us out of what God has given us in Christ. Yet God gives us all things that belong to Christ:

"He that spared not his own Son but delivered him up for us all, how shall he not with him also freely give us all things?" (Romans 8:32).

One chapter is not enough to do justice to the riches of the glory of the secret. An entire book could be written on this subject; however, we can outline some of these riches in the rest of this chapter.

The riches of the glory in the new man

The glory of the secret is having Christ in us. The riches of the glory of the secret refer to all that God has made Christ to be unto us. These are the depths of the secret. These great riches are to be found in the new man where all things new are Christ and are of God. For us, the new man lives in the riches of the glory where Christ is all and in all. The riches of the glory of the Great Secret are addressed to the new man.

Raised together and made alive together

When Christ was raised from the dead, we were raised with him. We were once spiritually dead but now we have been made alive in Christ as a new man created by God.

"Even when we were dead in sins, hath quickened us together
with Christ" (Ephesians 2:5)

Today, we are alive in Christ.

Seated in the heavenlies at the right hand of God

Jesus Christ was raised from the dead by the Father. After Jesus
Christ ascended, the Father sat him down at His right hand in
the heavenlies.

"Which He wrought in Christ, when He raised him from the
dead, and set *him* at His own right hand in the heavenly
places" (Ephesians 1:20)

The right hand of God is a figure of speech which means the
hand of blessing. We too have been made to sit down in the
heavenlies at the right hand of God.

"And hath raised *us* up together and made *us* sit together in
heavenly *places* in Christ Jesus" (Ephesians 2:6)

Our new man is seated in Christ in the heavenly places at the
right hand (blessing) of God where our Father's abundant
blessings are made to us. When Christ ascended, our new man
ascended with him. When he sat down at the right hand of the
Father, our new man sat down too. The words "heavenly places"
refer to a special place in the heavenlies where Christ sits far
above all at the very right hand of God.

Citizenship of the heavenly city

Prior to us being saved in Christ, we were citizens of this world,
alienated from God without hope and strangers to all the
promises of God. Now we have been reconciled to God. Now we
are in Christ and Christ has citizenship of many places including

the heavenly city where he will reign upon the throne of the Father. In our new created man we are the subject of all the promises of the hope in Christ for the called out ones in him.

"Now therefore ye are no more strangers and foreigners, but fellowcitizens with the saints, and of the household of God" (Ephesians 2:19).

and,

"But ye are come unto mount Sion, and unto the city of the living God, the heavenly Jerusalem, and to an innumerable company of angels,

To the general assembly and church of the firstborn, which are written in heaven, and to God the Judge of all, and to the spirits of just men made perfect" (Hebrews 12:22-23).

and,

"For our conversation [*"politeuma" means citizenship*] is in heaven; from whence also we look for the Saviour, the Lord Jesus Christ" (Philippians 3:20)

Our new man dwells in the heavenlies and is no stranger to all the blessings and promises of God to Christ and the called out ones. We are included by God Himself.

The seat of authority – far above all

As we have seen, Christ sat down at the right hand of the Father in a place that is far above all.

"Far above all principality, and power, and might, and dominion, and every name that is named, not only in this world, but also in that which is to come" (Ephesians 1:21)

The only one who is above Christ is our heavenly Father. Everything in creation is under his feet, and there is a time coming when every enemy shall be subject to him. Our new man is in Christ and is in this very same position as our Lord and Saviour Jesus Christ. We are sons together with him seated before our Father, and we have begun learning how to exercise this authority.

"....and set *him* at his own right hand in the heavenly *places*,

Far above all....

And hath put all *things* under his feet, and gave him *to be* the head over all *things* to the church,

Which is his body, the fulness of him that filleth all in all." (Ephesians 1:20-23)

Our new man sits in the same position as Christ sits today. The Adversary, the Devil, is under our feet and we have overcome his world because we have been born of God.

"For whatsoever is born of God overcometh the world, and this is the victory that overcometh the world, *even* our faith." (1 John 5:4)

We have the ascended, victorious, living Christ in us and we have begun growing up into him.

Completely complete in him

God declares that we are complete in Christ. This means that in the new man there is nothing lacking.

"And ye are complete in him, which is the head of all principality and power" (Colossians 2:10).

A physical baby is a complete physical package, but not yet fully grown. Likewise, even as a babe in Christ, we have the complete package, only that we are not yet fully grown up in all of what God has given to us in Christ. God is no respecter of persons. He did not give any more in the new nature to anyone in the Body of Christ. Rather, He gave to us all the same measure of the faith of Christ and the same spirit of Christ. The word complete here is actually emphasised so it literally means that we are all completely complete in Christ.

The righteousness of God

The glory of the Great Secret is so rich that you and I have been made the righteousness of God. This means that our new man is righteous as God is righteous: God has created the new man in this manner. God made Jesus Christ to be as sin, though he committed no sin: this was for us so that we in turn could be made into the righteousness of God.

> "For He hath made him *to be* sin for us, who knew no sin; that we might be made the righteousness of God in him."
> (2 Corinthians 5:21).

God created our new man in righteousness according to His own image:

> "And that ye put on the new man, which after God is created in righteousness and true holiness." (Ephesians 4:24).

This righteousness and this true holiness refer to the righteousness and holiness that belongs to God Himself, but also refer to the new man because the new man is God's work. In other words, God has written His righteousness and His holiness into the new man.

Conclusion

The above are some of the riches of the glory of the secret of the Christ in us. There are many more which our Father desires to make known.

Chapter 37: The future of the Great Secret (The hope of glory)

The hope of glory - looking into the future

One day, sometime in the future, the Great Secret will be fully completed. The words from Paul to the Colossians look forward into that future:

"......Christ in you, the hope of glory" (Colossians 1:27).

The phrase "the hope of glory" refers to the certainty of us obtaining the glory of our Lord Jesus Christ. This has been promised to us by God Himself:

"Whereunto He called you by our gospel to the obtaining of the glory of our Lord Jesus Christ. " (2 Thessalonians 2:14)

This is the future of the Great Secret. This is our future. The "Christ in you" is the spirit of Christ in you today. This is the incorruptible seed in you now that will later flourish into the full grown perfect man of Christ. Ephesians declares that the holy spirit in us is a token which will later be redeemed for the full purchased possession. The future of the Great Secret is a glorious one.

There is a future glory that will be revealed in us. This will occur when our Father finishes the work that He has started in us. Today, we are being fashioned into the image of His Son; in the future, we will obtain the glory that He gives to Jesus Christ as King of Kings and Lord of Lords. At some point, we will be glorified and it will be visible for all to see:

"When he shall [*have*] come to be glorified in his saints, and to be admired in all them that believe (because our testimony among you was believed in that day." (2 Thessalonians 1:10).

Men will admire the glory that the Father will place in us in that day. It will be evident for all to see. In Ephesians, we read that "we are to the praise of the glory of his grace" (Ephesians 1:6) and also that God's work is such "that we should be to the praise of his glory" (Ephesians 1:12). Our future inheritance, which refers to when we are fully grown up into Christ, will most definitely be to the praise of his glory. People will speak and sing praises to God's glory and the glory of His grace on account of what they will see in us. In the future, they will see the product of God's glorious work of grace in us. The Body of Christ will be an object lesson for the whole of mankind.

Changed into his glory in the future - a new glorious body

The hope of glory also includes a wonderful change that will be wrought in us when Jesus Christ returns:

"Who shall change our vile body, that it may be fashioned like unto his glorious body, according to the working whereby he is able even to subdue all things unto himself."
(Philippians 3:21)

The physical body that we have now is "vile" compared to the new glorious body that will be given to us at the return of Jesus Christ and our gathering together unto him. This new body is like the glorious body that Jesus Christ has today. One day we will be fully like him, and fully changed into his glory. We will be given a new glorious body.

Paul referred to this in 2 Corinthians when he said that if our earthly house of this tabernacle was dissolved we have a house (new body) reserved for us in the heavens.

"For we know that if our earthly house of *this* tabernacle were dissolved, we have a building of God, an house not made with hands, eternal in the heavens." (2 Corinthians 5:1)

Changed into his glory in the future - what is in the new body?

Within the new body will be a quickening or rather a life giving spirit and the glory of our Lord Jesus Christ.

"And so it is written, the first man Adam was made a living soul; the last Adam *was made* a quickening spirit....

And as we have borne the image of the earthy, we shall also bear the image of the heavenly." (1 Corinthians 15:45 and 49)

This glory is to be revealed in us:

"For I reckon that the sufferings of this present time *are* not worthy *to be compared* with the glory which shall be revealed in us." (Romans 8:18)

This glory in the future will be a life giving glory:

"For the earnest expectation of the creature waiteth for the manifestation of the sons of God.

For the creature was made subject to vanity, not willingly, but by reason of Him who hath subjected *the same* in hope,

Because the creature itself shall also be delivered from the bondage of corruption into the glorious liberty of the children of God." (Romans 8:19-21)

Here, the Word of God teaches that even the whole creation is waiting to be released into the liberty of our future glory. Today, the order of creation is one of decay over time; the order of creation in the future will be the exact opposite where it will be subject to a new life giving order. How great is this secret and our part in it.

New mind

Today, we have imperfections in our minds. We do not always think God's will. However, in the day that is coming, our minds will be fully perfected. We will have the perfect mind of Christ:

"For we know in part, and we prophesy in part.

But when that which is perfect is come, then that which is in part shall be done away.

.......but then shall I know even as also I am known."
(1 Corinthians 13:9,10 and 12)

In that day, we shall know fully know who we are in Christ just like the Father knows all about the new man which He has created. In an earlier chapter, we saw that the Great Secret was given by God for the obedience of believing. This is what He wants His children to believe. He has chosen His wise counsel for us. This counsel is the gospel of the glory of our Lord Jesus Christ in which we grow up into Christ in all things that he is.

The prize – the full stature of Christ

We have seen in earlier chapters how that in the future we shall be made fully like him. Our heavenly Father sees the finishing line of when we will have attained "the measure of the stature of the fulness of Christ" (Ephesians 4:13). Our heavenly Father will mature us into the fulness of Christ, the perfect man. We will be fully like Christ.

In the Great Secret, we died both to ourselves and the ways of this world in order that we might become the one new man in Christ and thereby live the Christ that Father has placed in us. We are then set on a road that ends with receiving the prize in the calling on high. At the gathering together we are made fully like him. This is the prize of the calling on high:

> "I press toward the mark for the prize of the high calling of God in Christ Jesus." (Philippians 3:14)

Joint Heirs

The riches of the glory of this secret also extend to our future inheritance. With Christ, we are joint heirs of all that the Father owns in creation. Paul told the Corinthians to realise that all things belong to the Body of Christ:

> "........ For all things are yours;

> Whether Paul, or Apollos, or Cephas, or the world, or life, or death, or things present, or things to come; all are yours;

> And ye are Christ's; and Christ *is* God's."
> (1 Corinthians 3:21-23)

We shall inherit all things.

> " .... That we are the children of God;

> And if children, then heirs; heirs of God, and joint heirs with Christ; if so be that we suffer with *him*, that we may be also glorified together." (Romans 8:16-17)

Forever with the Lord

One day the Lord Jesus Christ will descend from heaven and we shall meet him in the clouds of the heavens. In this way and from this point forward we shall be forever with the Lord.

"For the Lord shall descend from heaven with a shout, with the voice of the archangel, and with the trump of God: and the dead in Christ shall rise first:

Then we which are alive *and* remain shall be caught up together with them in the clouds, to meet the Lord in the air: and so shall we ever be with the Lord."
(1 Thessalonians 4:16-17)

Therefore, it is axiomatic that wherever the Lord goes in the future we will be with him. This is not difficult to understand when you realise that you are a joint heir with Christ and that the saints will judge the world. In all that Christ will do in the future we shall be with him.

The finished work

God has begun a good work in us already. We are being changed into Christ today.

"Being confident of this very thing, that He which hath begun a good work in you will perform *it* until the day of Jesus Christ." (Philippians 1:6)

God will continue this work until the day of Christ at which point He will stop. The reason for this is simply by that time He would have completed the Great Secret. In other words we would have been completely made like Christ. We will be like him for we shall see him as he is.

Conclusion

It is Christ in you the hope of his glory. One day, we will come into the glory of Jesus Christ who is the King of kings and the

Lord of lords.

"Beloved, now are we the sons of God, and it doth not yet appear what we shall be; but we know that, when he shall appear, we shall be like him; for we shall see him as he is." (1 John 3:2)

Part IX - The Great Secret and the Heart of Man

Chapter 38: The Great Secret and the heart of man

The next step for today

In the previous chapters we have seen how much God has done for all of us who are in the Body of Christ. Now, His desire is for all this grace to be alive in our hearts. He wants this so that we are truly connected with what He has given us. This requires that we become what the Word says we have spiritually in Christ. This means that we connect with it in the way we live our lives. This can only take place in our hearts and it can only be done when we believe what God has revealed for us in the Epistles.

Understanding the relationship between the heart and the Great Secret will open up the way further for us to grow up mightily into Christ. But to understand the heart we need to go back to the foundations of understanding laid down in the Old Testament.

Out of the heart are the issues of life

Whatever is in your heart will directly affect what happens in your life.

> "Keep thy heart with all diligence; for out of it *are* the issues of life." (Proverbs 4:23)

The phrase "the issues of life" refers to what is in your life, or what your life consists. Whatever is in our heart will also be manifest in our lives. This is a rule of life. We live our lives both in and from our hearts. If evil, lies and deception are in a man's heart, then evil, lies and deception will also be evident in the issues of his life. But, if love, honour, purity and godliness are in his heart, his life will reflect these qualities instead. This is a very powerful lesson for man to learn, especially when it comes to living the Christ in us.

Out of the abundance of the heart the mouth speaketh

Not only do the issues of life come from our hearts, but the heart determines what is spoken and how it is spoken:

> "....for out of the abundance of the heart the mouth speaketh." (Matthew 12:34b)

Jesus Christ taught that a man speaks out from the abundance of what is in his heart. Our speech is conditioned by what is in our hearts. If we have forgiveness, gentleness, mercy and forbearance, what we say and how we say it will not be harsh but rather forgiving and gentle and full of mercy. Whatever is in our hearts will also be in our speech. This is another powerful lesson.

The man of the heart

The person that you really are is exactly what is in your heart. Again, if there is love in your heart, you will be a loving person. If there is greed in your heart, you will have greedy traits in your personality and character. This principle was well known in the Old Testament:

> "For as he thinketh in his heart, so *is* he". (Proverbs 23:7)

What is in our heart determines who we are. In particular, the thoughts of our heart determine who we are. We all need to understand God's instruction about the man of the heart. Now here is our choice. After having been born from above, will we go on to become what Christ is, or will we turn away to grow into something else? This is what I call "The battle for the man of the heart". Our loving heavenly Father wants us, in our hearts, to grow into Christ, into his image; the Adversary wants the man of our heart to be fashioned according to this world which is in the Devil's image. What will you become?

Sadly, so many Christians, although they were made rich by God's abundant spiritual blessings in Christ, have since walked in the poverty of the Adversary's will and have further grown and matured to become the carnal man of the heart. However, God's will for us is that we go on to become the Christ man of the heart. Paul's prayer in Ephesians is that Christ may dwell in your heart by faith.

> "For this cause I bow my knees unto the Father of our Lord Jesus Christ...
>
> That Christ may dwell in your hearts by faith..."
> (Ephesians 3:14 and 17)

This is something far beyond God placing the spirit of His Son in us when we were born again. Rather, it is the reality of Christ living in our hearts. Many have been given the spirit of Christ by our Father, yet their hearts are set on carnal things and still sold out to sin. Yet, for others the realities of the spirit of Christ have taken root in their hearts so that they have become what has been written. Our intended destiny is that the man of our heart is Christ.

> "And because ye are sons, God hath sent forth the spirit of His Son into your hearts, crying, Abba, Father" (Galatians 4:6)

This is made possible when we believe the Word of God, especially that which is written to us in the Epistles. Now if Christ is in our hearts, then Christ will also be evident in both the life we live and how we live. The more Christ is in your heart, the more of your life's issues will be those of Christ.

Now to take this a step further, if you are thinking Christ's thoughts in your heart, then you are truly growing up into Christ. You are becoming what he is and thereby being perfected in him.

As a man thinks in his heart, so is he. Therefore think Christ. Think the Word of God and believe!! That is why it is a powerful thing, not just to have Christ in you by way of spirit but rather to have all of what Christ has been made unto you in your heart. The Word of God says that you will then become it; you will then speak it; and the issues of your life will then be those of Jesus Christ and the Father. What a powerful lesson!

Be renewed in the life of your mind

We can therefore now understand why Paul exhorted us to be renewed in the life of our mind:

"And be renewed in the spirit of your mind;

And that ye put on the new man, which after God is created in true righteousness and holiness." (Ephesians 4:23-24)

The phrase "spirit of your mind" is literally the life of your mind. Paul was referring to Christ dwelling in the heart so that the issues of our lives would be those belonging to Christ; and so that we would live the Christ life; and so that Christ would become the man of our heart. God has put the new man in us by way of the gift of holy spirit. We are now to put on that new man; we do this in our heart. It is no longer just resident in us as potential but instead we become the very new man that God has created by living the new nature in our heart.

God saved us when we were dead in sins. Today we are growing up into the head of the One Body, even into Christ in all things. Christ is the man of our heart.

When the Word of God addresses the man of the heart

Understanding these truths will open up the Word of God like never before. Many have struggled to understand why Paul would often write harsh things to the members of the Body of Christ.

Many have even denied that these are addressed to the church. So often God addresses His Word to the man of the heart and we need to understand this in order to handle the more difficult Scriptures honestly.

Paul spoke of some whose end is to be destruction:

"For many walk, of whom I have told you often, and now tell you even weeping, *that they are* the enemies of the cross of Christ:

Whose end is destruction, whose God *is their* belly, and *whose* glory *is* in their shame, who mind earthly things." (Philippians 3:18-19)

Here, Paul was not teaching the Philippians about the unbelievers, those who had not accepted Christ. Of course the unsaved were carnally minded, just like the sky is blue! Of course they were on the road to destruction and perdition. The Philippians did not need to be told that for they already knew it by experience; for they themselves were once unsaved and carnally minded. Rather, Paul was here talking about those who were saved, but the man of their heart had become the enemy of the cross of Christ. This was because they did not walk in believing obedience according to God's Word. The destruction that Paul was pointing to was not that they would lose their salvation but rather that the carnal man of their heart that they had so magnified would be destroyed by God.

Man's works are from the heart. They are a direct reflection of the man of the heart, and thereby cannot be divorced from the man of the heart. Take a look at Corinthians, where Paul reveals the future of the man of the heart and his works:

"Every man's work shall be made manifest: for the day shall declare it, because it shall be revealed by fire; and the fire shall try every man's work of what sort it is.

If any man's work abide which he hath built thereupon, he shall receive a reward.

If any man's work shall be burned, he shall suffer loss: but he himself shall be saved; yet so as by fire."
(1 Corinthians 3: 13-15)

Everyone who has accepted Christ will be saved, even if some will need to be saved yet so as by fire. However, here in Corinthians we learn that the man of the heart of some will be destroyed.

"If any man defile the temple of God, him shall God destroy; for the temple of God is holy, which *temple* ye are."
(1 Corinthians 3:17)

The word "him" refers to the man of the heart. A born again believer who has become an idolater will be saved but the idolatrous man of his heart will be destroyed. This is simple. However, for all of us who have become in our hearts what Christ is, we shall receive rewards. The man of our heart is Christ, and there are rewards awaiting us. Praise God.

The battle for the heart

Our understanding of the Great Secret in Christ would not be complete without understanding the great revelation about the heart in the context of our growing into Christ. Many of the scriptures in the epistles refer to the man of the heart and as such are about the heart. The reason why God gave man freewill was so that man in his heart could make the decision to love God and obey His will.

Your heart has an important role in determining who you are, what you are, what you speak and what the issues in your life are. God looks on the heart

"....for man looketh on the outward appearance, but the Lord looketh on the heart" (1 Samuel 16:7)

God wants the man of your heart to be the Christ in you so that you may do the will of God from your innermost being, so that you may prove the will of God in your life.

"For this cause I bow my knees unto the Father of our Lord Jesus Christ...

That Christ may dwell in your hearts by faith..."
(Ephesians 3:14 and 17)

This is one of the most important keys in how to live the Great Secret.

Chapter 39: What the Great Secret looks like on the outside

Simply, the Great Secret looks like Christ on the outside but what does this really mean?

Fruit of the spirit

The Word of God declares that there are nine fruits of the spirit:

> "But the fruit of the spirit is love, joy, peace, longsuffering, gentleness, goodness, faith,
>
> Meekness, temperance: against such there is no law." (Galatians 5:22-23)

Notice that these are not fruit of good works but fruit of the spirit. When you walk by the spirit, you will produce and cultivate the fruit of the spirit. We have seen in an earlier chapter that walking by the spirit is literally walking in the new nature. It is the walk of the new spiritual man which God has created that produces and cultivates spiritual fruit. In turn, walking in the spirit allows the new man to grow. This growth produces and cultivates the fruit of the spirit in our lives.

> "But speaking the truth in love, may grow up into him in all things, which is the head, *even* Christ" (Ephesians 4:15)

When the fruit of the spirit is cultivated in your life, then you are truly growing up into the new man. This means that you are growing into Christ, the head of the One Body.

The nature of God

The fruit of the spirit describes the nature of our Father. God acts in love and kindness. He is peaceful, longsuffering and patient. When we produce the fruit of the spirit, we are growing up into the head of the Body. In other words we are being conformed to and changed into the image of Christ who in turn is the image of God. We then reflect the very nature of God in how we live.

> "For whom He did foreknow, he also did predestinate *to be* conformed to the image of his Son, that he might be the firstborn among many brethren." (Romans 8:29)

The heart

Producing fruit of the spirit takes place in the heart. The new man is already in us because of the spirit of Christ which dwells in us. However, the place where the new man grows is in our hearts. This is the place where we are transformed into Christ. The fruit of the spirit is part of the Great Secret in this way. The more fruit in our lives, the more we can walk in Christ.

The fruit of the spirit enables you both to see and act as Jesus Christ sees and acts. Love, kindness, joy, peace etc are all component parts of the walk of Jesus Christ. Without peace, it is impossible to walk in peace. Likewise, a person must have love in his heart in order to love. This principle is relevant to all nine fruit of the spirit.

Your spiritual workout

The fruit of the spirit is the fruit of the spirit of Christ in you. Another way of looking at this is to understand that it is your spiritual workout in the 'Christ gym'. Here, you will develop the 'spiritual muscle' of the Christ in you so that you can grow up into him and walk like him. The fruit of the spirit enables you both to see and act as Jesus Christ sees and acts. It is an integral part of God's plan for the Great Secret being unfolded in your life.

Reflecting the divine nature

In Christ, we are partakers of God's own nature. This is cultivated within us so that we act and behave in the same way as God:

> "Whereby are given unto us exceeding great and precious promises: that by these ye might be partakers of the divine nature, having escaped the corruption that is in the world through lust." (2 Peter 1:4)

Producing fruit of the spirit involves being a partaker of God's own nature. Through bearing the fruit of the spirit, we reflect God's nature and we are growing up in the Christ in us. These truths will become plainer and more real to us when we understand more about how the Great Secret has effect on the heart of man. The more Christ becomes the man of your heart, the more you will be living the Great Secret as God intended in this Age of Grace.

The fruit of the spirit is part of God's big picture in the Great Secret.

Chapter 40: Let us go on unto perfection

Being perfected in Christ

In the Great Secret we see how the Father has placed the perfect spirit of Christ in us. However, God's will is that after receiving this perfect spirit in us, we should now go on to become perfect in our hearts as Christ is also perfect.

> "Therefore leaving the principles of the doctrine of Christ, let us go on unto perfection [Gr. *teleiotes*]...." (Hebrews 6:1a)

In other words, God wants us to go on to be perfected or become perfect before Him. Father has planted the seed of Christ in us. Now, in growing up into him we become perfect in him.

To understand this more clearly, we need to realise that God is talking about perfection being wrought in our hearts. There are three basic Greek words for perfection used in the New Testament:

Akribos - meaning perfect in the sense of being accurate, precise or exact

Artios or *Exartiso* - meaning perfect in the sense of being fully equipped or fully furnished

Teleios or *Teleiotes* - meaning perfect in the sense of being completed, finished, brought to full maturity

These words are very significant to our understanding of the Great Secret. Our Father wants us to have accurate understanding of the Great Secret, and thereby be fully equipped so that we may be presented perfect and complete in the Great Secret in Christ.

In the Epistles, there are a number of particular areas that God tells us are to be perfected in our hearts. Let's take a look at these.

Standing perfect and complete in all the will of God – Epaphras

Epaphras lived in Colossae in the first century and he knew that such perfection was available in the Great Secret.

> "Epaphras, who is *one* of you, a servant of Christ, saluteth you, always labouring fervently for you in prayers, that ye may stand perfect [Gr. *teleios*] and complete in all the will of God." (Colossians 4:12)

The Great Secret is the will of God for the entire Church. Epaphras prayed that the Christians in Colossae would stand perfected and complete in their hearts in all of the riches of the Great Secret.

Paul and his fellow workers in the ministry preached the Great Secret so that they could present every Christian perfect in Christ:

> "Whom we preach, warning every man, and teaching every man in all wisdom; that we may present every man perfect [Gr. *teleios*] in Christ Jesus" (Colossians 1:28)

Paul was building Christ in their hearts. Christ is perfect and every part of Christ that lives in your heart means that you are being perfected in him.

Truly is the love of God being brought to perfection in you

As we walk faithfully upon the Word of God, then the love of

God is being brought to perfection in our hearts:

> "But whoso keepeth his word, in him verily is the love of God perfected [Gr. *teleioo*]: hereby know we that we are in him." (1 John 2:5)

To keep His word means to do it. When we actually carry out what His Word says, then the love of God is brought to perfection in the person that you grow to be. Our destiny is the perfection of the Lord Jesus Christ, the perfect man.

Perfecting holiness in you

As we grow up into the purity of Christ in all things, then holiness is also brought to perfection in our hearts:

> "Having therefore these promises, dearly beloved, let us cleanse ourselves from all filthiness of the flesh and spirit, perfecting [Gr. *epiteleo*] holiness in the fear of God." (2 Corinthians 7:1)

We must rightly divide the difference between the holy nature of the spirit in us (holy spirit) and who we are in our hearts. God says that we are to become what is holy; this takes place in our hearts so that what we do and what we speak is holy. Certainly, because of God's grace, a person can have the gift of holy spirit in him and his heart is unholy. Father's desire is to see our hearts being perfected in holiness. That's when God's holiness is brought to perfection in us, in the person we are in our hearts.

God's strength is being perfected in you

The work of God in us is more powerful than any power that the Adversary can muster against us. As we die to our old nature and become alive to what God has made us to be in Christ, then God's strength is brought to perfection in our hearts and lives:

"And he said unto me, My grace is sufficient for thee: for my strength is made perfect [Gr. *teleioo*] in weakness. Most gladly therefore will I rather glory in my infirmities, that the power of Christ may rest upon me." (2 Corinthians 12:9)

God's strength in us increases and prevails in our lives when we cease relying on ourselves and look only to God. Therefore, God continues to give us of His strength. We avail ourselves of this strength when we love Him and live in what He provides rather than rest in our own strengths. Then God's strength is perfected in our hearts and lives in us because He is then at work in us to will and to do of His good pleasure.

Perfectly equipped with the knowledge of the Great Secret

The will of God for your life is that you are fully equipped with the full knowledge of the Great Secret which leads to the unity of the faith, and which leads to the true knowledge of who the Son of God is, which leads to the perfect man, and which leads to the full measure of Christ's stature. The ministries of apostles, prophets, pastors and teachers are given by God to the Body of Christ. The reasons why God has given these to us are:

"For the perfecting [Gr. *katartismos*] of the saints, for the work of the ministry, for the edifying of the body of Christ:

Till we all come in the unity of the faith, and of the knowledge of the Son of God, unto a perfect [Gr. *teleios*] man, unto the measure of the stature of the fulness of Christ" (Ephesians 4:12-13).

The word "perfecting" here is "*katartismos*" which refers to the fully equipping of the saints. This really means completely furnishing the saints with the Word of God concerning the Great Secret.

The context of the Epistles is the Great Secret. When you read the Epistles in the light of this understanding you will gain a greater depth of what Paul was teaching and writing about. When he wrote to the Thessalonians, he told them that he wanted to meet with them so that through his ministry, he could fill up what was lacking in their knowledge and believing so that they would be fully equipped and therefore lack nothing regarding "comprehending" the breadth, length, depth and height of the Great Secret. He wanted to supply them with a greater knowledge and understanding than they had gained so far:

> "Night and day praying exceedingly that we might see your face, and might perfect [*katartiso*] that which is lacking in your faith." (1 Thessalonians 3:10)

Paul wrote to the Corinthians telling them that they should be perfect. What he was really saying was that they were to be perfectly equipped with all of the Word and all of the knowledge regarding the Great Secret:

> "Finally, brethren, farewell. Be perfect [*katartizo*], be of good comfort, be of one mind, live in peace; and the God of love and peace shall be with you." (2 Corinthians 13:11)

Today, it is God's will that we are to be fully equipped with the Word of God regarding the Great Secret. He wants us to fully know and be fully equipped with this knowledge so that we may live by the faith of Jesus Christ which is the Great Secret.

> "I am crucified with Christ: nevertheless I live; yet not I, but Christ liveth in me: and the life which I now live in the flesh I live by the faith of the Son of God, who loved me, and gave himself for me." (Galatians 2:20)

Being perfected though not yet fully perfected

Today, we are being perfected but so far we are only partly perfected. We have the perfect spirit of Christ in us. The new man in us is perfect. However, our growing up into the new man in our hearts has only just begun and we have not yet put on everything that is Christ. Today, it is our joy to learn of the perfection of Jesus Christ, who is the perfect man. It is also our present joy to begin to grow up into his perfection. In our hearts, we have arrived at the foot of the stature of the fulness of Jesus Christ, but we are not yet fully grown into his perfection. At the return of Jesus Christ we will be fully perfected; God will complete the work of us being perfected in Christ:

> "But when that which is perfect is come, then that which is in part shall be done away." (1 Corinthians 13:10)

In that day, we will be fully perfected in Christ. Then, we will have perfect bodies and perfect hearts and minds. In that day we will be fully grown into the measure of the stature of the fulness of Christ. Today, as we walk faithfully in the Great Secret, we are being perfected in more and more aspects of Jesus Christ; more and more, we are being perfected in our hearts in the "all things" that he is. However, the perfection that has been wrought in us so far will continue throughout all eternity. Paul pursued this perfection of growing up into Christ in his own walk:

> "Not as though I had already attained, either were already perfect: but I follow after, if that I may apprehend that for which also I am apprehended of Christ Jesus.
>
> Brethren, I count not myself to have apprehended: but *this* one thing *I do*, forgetting those things which are behind, and reaching forth unto those things which are before,

I press toward the mark for the prize of the high calling of
God in Christ Jesus.

Let us therefore, as many as be perfect, be thus minded….."
(Philippians 3:12-15a)

Let's understand this important section of scripture. Paul knew
that he hadn't been fully perfected yet into the all things of
Christ. He was certainly on the way, and many aspects of the all
things of Christ had already been perfected in his heart. In his
heart he was growing up into the head, even Christ himself. He
pursued this perfecting with great vigour allowing God to work in
him mightily to that end. The word "apprehend" here is
"*katalambano*" in the Greek and as we have seen in an earlier
chapter, it means to lay hold on. Jesus Christ laid hold on us so
that we might become what he is. This is the prize of the high
calling. The transformation has already started today. God's
commandment is that the mature in the Great Secret are to think
like this. God is at work in us according to His good pleasure:

"Being confident of this very thing, that he which hath begun
a good work in you will perform *it* until the day of Jesus
Christ" (Philippians 1:6)

Right now, God is perfecting you in Christ and He will continue
to perform this work in you until the gathering together at which
point He will finish the work.

"So Christ was once offered to bear the sins of many; and
unto them that look for him shall he appear the second time
without sin unto salvation." (Hebrews 9:28)

Walking perfectly in Christ

Our Father's will for us is that we also walk perfectly in Christ.
He is bringing us to the perfection of His son Christ as He
nurtures us and grows us up into him in all things. His will is that

we are perfectly equipped with all the knowledge of the Great Secret so that we can walk in the accurate and precise knowledge of this wonderful revelation.

> "See then that ye walk circumspectly [*"akribos" meaning accurate, precise and perfect*], not as fools, but as wise,
>
> Redeeming the time, because the days are evil.
>
> Wherefore be ye not unwise, but understanding what the will of the Lord *is*". (Ephesians 5:15-17)

God wants us to walk perfectly before Him. He wants us to walk accurately in the Great Secret. This is the essence of the word *"akribos"* which is here translated circumspectly. He wants us to know the score both as to the days being evil and the truth of the revelation of the Great Secret which is far greater and more powerful in our lives. He wants us to walk in the accuracy and integrity of the wonderful revelation of the Great Secret.

Conclusion

In the Great Secret we are being brought to perfection. After receiving the perfect spirit of Christ in us, it is God's will that we should now go on to become perfect in our hearts as Christ is also perfect.

> "Howbeit we speak wisdom among them that are perfect [*teleios*]: yet not the wisdom of this world, nor of the princes of this world, that come to nought" (1 Corinthians 2:6)

In the unfolding of this Great Secret, we have come "unto the perfect man" of Ephesians 4:13 who is Christ, the Son of God. We are becoming the perfect man of the heart in Christ. This is

God's will. So great is the salvation of God through Jesus Christ. We are to know God's will and walk circumspectly having been fully equipped with true knowledge of the Great Secret. This is God's will for us today.

Chapter 41: Walking in the Great Secret

The walk of the new man

The new man is a godly man, someone who walks in the wisdom of God. It is not God's will to simply acquire the knowledge of this secret and then sit on it and live like the unbelieving nations in the vanity of their minds.

> "This I say therefore, and testify in the Lord, that ye henceforth walk not as other Gentiles walk, in the vanity of their mind,
>
> Having the understanding darkened, being alienated from the life of God through the ignorance that is in them, because of the blindness of their heart...
>
> .. But ye have not so learned Christ....
>
> ...put on the new man, which after God is created in righteousness and true holiness." (Ephesians 4:17-24)

We walk in the Great Secret by literally walking in the new man that God has created us to be in Christ. This involves putting on the new man in our hearts.

The key is recognizing that it is Christ in you and then going on to believe all that the Epistles declare about this Christ in you. Paul prayed that the believers in Colossae would be filled with knowledge and understanding of God's will as it is revealed in the Great Secret.

> "For this cause we also, since the day we heard *it*, do not cease to pray for you, and to desire that ye might be filled

with the knowledge of his will in all wisdom and spiritual understanding;

That ye might walk worthy of the Lord unto all pleasing, being fruitful in every good work, and increasing in the knowledge of God" (Colossians 1:9-10)

When you believe what is written about you in the Great Secret as revealed in the Epistles, you receive the wisdom and knowledge of his will concerning your walk. Then you are able to walk in the Great Secret which pleases God and this involves being fruitful in every good work. You are then walking in Christ as he himself walks.

All of the riches of the secret are addressed to the new man and are accessed via the new nature. As you walk in the new man you will avail yourself of all the exceeding great and precious promises that are available today in the Great Secret.

Recognizing the One Body of Christ

Walking spiritually in the Great Secret also requires our thinking and behaviour to be in accordance with the One Body of Christ.

The Corinthians failed many times to walk in accordance with the truths of the One Body. In the first letter to the Corinthians, Paul would reprove them many times about this. They did not recognize the One Body and would divide it up in their own carnal thinking; one person would say that they were a follower of Paul, another of Apollos and so on. Paul warned them how they should take care in building the Body of Christ and how that God would destroy any man who defiles it.

Paul also reproved the Corinthians about fornication being a sin both against the physical body and against the One Body of Christ. With regards to the breaking of bread in remembrance of the Lord, he warned them that many did not discern the Body of Christ and behaved as if the One Body never existed. Some of the

Christians in Corinth acted selfishly regarding shared meals; in fact, they did not share but kept to their own. Paul had to remind them also that the use of the manifestations of holy spirit (speaking in tongues, interpretation of tongues and word of prophecy) in the fellowship meetings was for the building up of the One Body of Christ. In so many ways the Corinthian believers had shown themselves to be walking carnally and not according to the revelation of the Great Secret concerning the One Body of Christ.

Today, every Christian should examine themselves as to whether they are walking in accordance with the One Body of Christ.

Spiritual abilities

The ability to do all the things of the new man is resident within the spirit of Christ in you. Paul would say that he can do all things through Christ who strengthened him.

"I can do all things through Christ which strengtheneth me."
(Philippians 4:13)

Interestingly, we are to grow up into Christ the head in all things. These "all things" of Christ refer to both the all things that the perfect man is in nature and the all things that the perfect man can do. The word "strengthen" in the Greek is "*endunamoo*" and this literally means to be given everything required so that the job can be done. All of this comes from the Great Secret of Christ within.

The new man can do all the instructions that are listed in the Epistles. In the following list are pointers for you to make conscious decisions to walk this way because you can do so in the new nature. God says that you are to do it because you can do it. In other words you are able; you have everything that you need to get the job done because it is Christ in you.

The walk of the new man in Ephesians 4 and 5

"That ye put off concerning the former conversation the old man, which is corrupt according to the deceitful lusts;

And be renewed in the spirit of your mind;

And that ye put on the new man, which after God is created in righteousness and true holiness.

Wherefore putting away lying, speak every man truth with his neighbour: for we are members one of another.

Be ye angry, and sin not: let not the sun go down upon your wrath:

Neither give place to the devil.

Let him that stole steal no more: but rather let him labour, working with *his* hands the thing which is good, that he may have to give to him that needeth.

Let no corrupt communication proceed out of your mouth, but that which is good to the use of edifying, that it may minister grace unto the hearers.

And grieve not the holy Spirit of God, whereby ye are sealed unto the day of redemption.

Let all bitterness, and wrath, and anger, and clamour, and evil speaking, be put away from you, with all malice:

And be ye kind one to another, tenderhearted, forgiving one another, even as God for Christ's sake hath forgiven you.

Be ye therefore followers of God, as dear children;

And walk in love, as Christ also hath loved us, and hath given himself for us an offering and a sacrifice to God for a sweetsmelling savour.

But fornication, and all uncleanness, or covetousness, let it not be once named among you, as becometh saints;

Neither filthiness, nor foolish talking, nor jesting, which are not convenient: but rather giving of thanks."
(Ephesians 4:22-5:4)

The walk of the new man in Romans 12

"I beseech you therefore, brethren, by the mercies of God, that ye present your bodies a living sacrifice, holy, acceptable unto God, *which is* your reasonable service.

And be not conformed to this world: but be ye transformed by the renewing of your mind, that ye may prove what *is* that good, and acceptable, and perfect, will of God.

For I say, through the grace given unto me, to every man that is among you, not to think *of himself* more highly than he ought to think; but to think soberly, according as God hath dealt to every man the measure of faith.

For as we have many members in one body, and all members have not the same office:

So we, *being* many, are one body in Christ, and every one members one of another.

Having then gifts differing according to the grace that is given to us, whether prophecy, *let us prophesy* according to the proportion of faith;

Or ministry, *let us wait* on *our* ministering: or he that teacheth, on teaching;

Or he that exhorteth, on exhortation: he that giveth, *let him do it* with simplicity; he that ruleth, with diligence; he that sheweth mercy, with cheerfulness.

Let love be without dissimulation. Abhor that which is evil; cleave to that which is good.

Be kindly affectioned one to another with brotherly love; in honour preferring one another;

Not slothful in business; fervent in spirit; serving the Lord;

Rejoicing in hope; patient in tribulation; continuing instant in prayer;

Distributing to the necessity of saints; given to hospitality.

Bless them which persecute you: bless, and curse not.

Rejoice with them that do rejoice, and weep with them that weep.

Be of the same mind one toward another. Mind not high things, but condescend to men of low estate. Be not wise in your own conceits.

Recompense to no man evil for evil. Provide things honest in the sight of all men.

If it be possible, as much as lieth in you, live peaceably with all men.

Dearly beloved, avenge not yourselves, but *rather* give place unto wrath: for it is written, Vengeance *is* mine; I will repay, saith the Lord.

Therefore if thine enemy hunger, feed him; if he thirst, give him drink: for in so doing thou shalt heap coals of fire on his head.

Be not overcome of evil, but overcome evil with good." (Romans 12:1-21)

Conclusion

When your walk is like the above Scriptures, you can then avail yourself of the greatness of the secret. Paul spoke plainly because you can do all these things because it is Christ in you.

The new man does not lie, but always speaks the truth. In the new man anger is kept under control, and there is no place for the adversary, no foothold for him whatsoever, for you are a conqueror in the new nature. The new man works honestly and gives to the needy. All the words from the mouth of the new man minister grace and kindness to the hearers. The new man does not grieve God. There is no bitterness or clamour or shouting, but rather there is kindness and forgiveness. The new nature is like God. The new man walks in love and glorifies God.

All of these things are not addressed to the old man but to the new man in Christ. Therefore, you should never try to get the old fleshly man to do these things, but you are to rely on the new man which God has created. Moreover, you can look at these things with trust, believing and confidence that you can do them and will do them because the Christ in you gives you everything that you need to get the task done. These things are to characterize your walk. You are to be concerned that your walk is like this. You are to pursue these things and maintain good works.

The power is in the new man. The new man taps into all the greatness of the secret. Instead of vanity of the mind we are renewed in the life of the mind. The new man has been created in righteousness and true holiness in the image of God. Instead of vanity and strife, you walk in love instead. You live the truth in the love of God so that you may grow up into him in all things.

Part X - The Great Secret and the Purpose of the Ages

Chapter 42: The administrations of God's households and the history of the Great Secret

Different peoples and different times

It is a common but severe mistake to think that the entire Bible is written about the Church. Many teachers of the Word of God have stumbled at this very hurdle and in so doing have made the Word of God of none effect. However, in order to handle the Word of God accurately, honestly and with the integrity that it deserves, we must clearly recognise that God has addressed different people at different times. These addresses are contained in the Bible. Each time period has its own particulars that are different from other ages. In rightly dividing between these different ages, we can more fully appreciate the revelation of the Great Secret.

We should take great care in addressing the Church today with what God has addressed to Israel in the Old Testament. Furthermore, we should honour God regarding what is written in the Four Gospels. Most of what is written in these books was written about a time before Jesus had accomplished his work, and before the revelation of the Great Secret. Failure to recognise this will cause no end of confusion in understanding the Word of God. Therefore, we need to be careful that we do not rob the Gospels of their very special context, and thereby be guilty of perverting our Father's Word.

However, at the same time, some of the Word of God spans more than one age and more than one people. For example, we should love God with all our heart, mind, soul and strength. This was true in the Age of the Law under Moses and it is true today in the Age of Grace, in which we now live. However, some of the Word of God is addressed directly to only one group of people and declares God's will for that particular people in that particular time period. For example, the Great Secret is addressed to the Church of the One Body and not the Old Testament believers in Israel. Therefore, the Great Secret cannot be read into the Age of the Law because it was not available then. Likewise, there are certain things of the Age of the Law that should not be read into the present. Today, in the Age of Grace, we are not justified (made righteous) by the works of the Law, whereas believers in Moses' day would have been righteous if they carried out the Law. Look at the difference between what is written in the Old Testament and what is written in the Epistles. In the Old Testament, we read

"And it shall be our righteousness, if we observe to do all these commandments before the Lord our God, as he hath commanded us." (Deuteronomy 6:25)

It is true that in the Age of the Law, the works of the Law were righteousness to Israel. However, in the Age of Grace, God commands that "Christ *is* the end of the law for righteousness to every one that believeth." (Romans 10:4). Unlike in the Age of the Law, no man today in this Age of Grace is justified (made righteous) by the works of the Law. So, in the Epistles we read:

"Knowing that a man is not justified by the works of the law, but by the faith of Jesus Christ… for by the works of the law shall no flesh be justified." (Galatians 2:16)

The teachings of the Great Secret take a unique place in our Bibles; they are revealed only in the Epistles. This knowledge cannot be found in the Four Gospels, neither in the Old Testament scriptures such as Exodus, Deuteronomy, Isaiah, Ezekiel, Daniel etc because the Great Secret belongs to the Age of Grace. The secret is directly addressed to the One Body of Christ today, not to the Israel of the Old Testament.

Three groups of people in seven ages

In God's eyes, there are three groups of people spoken of in the Bible (Jews, Gentiles and the Church of God):

"Give none offence, neither to the Jews, nor to the Gentiles, nor to the Church of God." (1 Corinthians 10:32)

There are different sub sets of these peoples but all come under one of these broad headings. There are also at least seven different ages in which God deals with mankind. One of these is the Age of Grace or the Age of the Great Secret in which we now live. If we understand these different ages, then we can then go on to appreciate the time setting of the Great Secret. This will enable us to better understand the Great Secret in its special position in the unfolding of God's plans for mankind and the world in relation to His Son, our Lord Jesus Christ.

The seven ages of God's dealings with man are:

1. Original Paradise or Eden. To fulfil His plan of the ages, God has worked with man in a number of different administrations beginning with Adam in the Age of the Original Paradise. In this age, God spoke of Jesus Christ as the promised seed (Genesis 3:15).

2. After this time came the Patriarchal Administration. During this administration, there was no written Word of God in scrolls or in book form but the Word was written in the heavens. In the Patriarchal Age, there were men of God such as Noah, Elijah, and Abraham.

3. Then came the Administration of the Law which was given to Moses.

4. The Christ Administration. Jesus Christ came to Israel to confirm the promises that God had made to the fathers (Romans 15:8).

5. The Age of Grace or the Age of the Great Secret. Paul had received this administration for the entire Church of this period, which includes us today (Ephesians 3:2, Colossians 1:25-27, 1 Corinthians 19:17). In this administration, God's people become the one new man which is the One Body of Christ. This had been kept a secret, hid in God from all previous ages and generations.

6. The Christ Appearing Administration. This age begins with Christ gathering up the Church (2 Thessalonians 2:1-17) which then heralds the Day of the Lord.

7. The Glory Administration of the New Heavens and the New Earth (2 Corinthians 12:1-4, Revelation 21:1)

To understand the Scriptures properly, we must recognise these different ages and also understand how the Scriptures fit into the framework of these different times. God's timing is perfect. He reveals His will and He works His plan of the ages after the counsel of His own will.

"Oikonomia"

The Greek word *"oikonomia"* has been translated as dispensation and fellowship in our Bibles but it literally means household administration as we have seen in earlier chapters. However, this word is significant in two ways: firstly, it refers to how Father wants His affairs governed in His household; secondly, it refers to the period of time or how long that particular administration lasts for in God's plan of the ages.

In Ephesians 3:9, Paul declares that his ministry was to make all men see what is the administration (Gr. *oikonomia*) of the Great Secret. This refers to both the time setting of the administration of the Great Secret and how it is to be governed.

In the Old Testament, the prophets saw the sufferings of Christ (as shown in the Four Gospels) and the glory that is to come (as shown in the Book of Revelation). They also prophesied of the grace that should fill these two time extremes, but they could not understand the time gap between the sufferings and the glory because the Great Secret of this period was hid in God and not revealed until God had showed Paul. It was hid from all ages and generations. This means that you cannot find it in the Old Testament - it was not hid within the scriptures but rather it was hid in God himself. Paul declared to the Corinthians that an entire administration (Gr. *oikonomia*) was committed to him by God:

> ".... A dispensation [Gr. *oikonomia*] of the gospel is committed unto me." (1 Corinthians 9:17)

Paul was referring to the administration of the Great Secret, which was committed unto him. He revealed the entire scope of this administration.

The Church of the One Body of Christ

It is a startling truth to read in God's Word that the church in this Age of Grace (*ekklesia* - those who are called out to become the One Body of Christ) was kept a secret until it was revealed to the Apostle Paul. Following on from this, it is even more startling to realise that the church of the Four Gospel period (i.e. those called out during the time when Jesus Christ was on earth) should not be confused with the church of the One Body, for the latter was kept a secret. If it was a secret that God had hid in Himself, then it could not have existed during the period recorded in the Four Gospels when Jesus Christ was on earth. Therefore, there is great danger of wrongly dividing the Word if we get these two different callings mixed up.

What was written in the Four Gospels was about those called out at that time. It could not be directly referring to those called out to become the One Body of Christ for God had kept this later calling a secret hid in God Himself. However, many of those who were called out during Jesus Christ's presence on earth were also later to learn about a different calling in the Age of Grace, under the new revelation that was given to Paul. The greater calling would arrive for many as unfolded in the epistles of Paul.

Another interesting aspect of all this is that those called out in the Old Testament and Gospel period were to be the bride of Christ. However, we have been called out not to be part of the bride of Christ but to be part of the Great Secret, the One Body of Christ, as part of the bridegroom. Moreover, the church of the Great Secret is one new man in Christ and as such is not two, like the bride and bridegroom. Rather, we are one where Christ is simply in all and is all. There is no Israel, no male, no female, no bond nor free, but rather there is Christ who is all and in all. This is an entirely different calling and was hid in God until He revealed it to the Apostle Paul. The bride of Christ was never a secret. However, the calling to the one new man, the One Body of Christ, the church of the Great Secret, was indeed a secret that had not been revealed until Paul's ministry. It is important for all Christians today to understand how God differentiates between all these things. Equally, if any Christian wishes to remain ignorant, then they are in danger of wrongly dividing the Word of God and thereby standing unapproved before God.

Christ is the head of the Body. Physically, Christ is in heaven, in the holiest of all. Physically, we the members of that Body are here upon earth. However, spiritually we are one with Christ in the heavenlies, far above all in heaven's holiest of all.

Sadly, there has been a wholesale disregard of the Epistles by many Christians. This has had the effect of shutting off the knowledge of the riches of the Great Secret of Christ and the Church. It is not God's will that any member of the One Body of Christ should be spiritually anaemic or destroyed through lack of knowledge. Jesus Christ shed his blood so that the riches recorded in the Epistles could be given unto us and made known. It is not logical that man should ever hold the Epistles in less regards than the Gospels. This is a trick of the Adversary. To unlearned ears, it sounds right that we should hold the words of Jesus Christ in the Gospels higher than Paul's words in the Epistles. However, the truth is that both are equally from God and Jesus Christ died so that the greater could come of which he could not speak about in the Four Gospels. It is therefore a great dishonour to the blood that Jesus Christ spilt to lower the spiritual riches in the Epistles. He shed his blood so that these riches could be showered upon us in abundance.

The Four Gospels document the life, death, and resurrection of our Lord Jesus Christ. He came as Israel's King, but they rejected and killed him. The Epistles of Paul document the riches that God has accomplished for us through the work of Jesus Christ. These could not be made known until after the death, resurrection and ascension of our Lord Jesus Christ. Therefore, the Four Gospels document the life and prophecies of Jesus Christ but the Epistles document the riches that God has accomplished for us through the work of Jesus Christ.

The exceeding great and precious promises in this administration

In other ages, such as the Age of the Law in which Moses lived, the exceeding great and precious promises in Christ were not available. In addition, we should understand that in that time period such promises in Christ were not even known about.

> "But as it is written, Eye hath not seen, nor ear heard, neither have entered into the heart man, the things which God hath prepared for them that love him". (1 Corinthians 2:9).

Even during the Gospel period, when Jesus Christ was upon earth, these promises were not known about. At that time, it was unheard of that we would ever be seated in the heavenlies, far above all at the right hand of God in Christ. It was not known that we would be joint heirs with Christ and that we would obtain the very glory of our Lord Jesus Christ, who is King of Kings and Lord of Lords. The one new man was not available. It was never perceived that we would actually be changed into the same image of his glory. The riches of Christ were not available. It was not known that we would be filled with all the fulness of God in Christ, and that we would be completely complete in him as we are today. All these things belong to the Age or Administration of Grace in which we now live. God says that He had kept this Great Secret hid in Himself and it was past finding out by man, until He should reveal it.

The purpose of the ages

In Ephesians, Paul speaks of the eternal purpose. This phrase literally means the purpose of the ages. The Greek word *"aion"* means an age or a period of time.

> "To the intent that now unto the principalities and powers in heavenly *places* might be known by the church the manifold wisdom of God,
>
> According to the eternal purpose which he purposed in Christ Jesus our Lord" (Ephesians 3:10-11).

The purpose of all ages is for God to dwell in man and this is God in Christ in you. We are being "builded together for an habitation of God through the spirit" (Ephesians 2:22). For us, who are the subjects of the Great Secret, we are growing into a holy temple for the Father to dwell in.

The Great Secret is both individual (Christ in you) and collective (the Temple of the One Body of Christ). We have been created as one new man in which all things are Christ. We are growing up into the head of the One Body, even into Christ in all things. The Temple of God is a living man, the ascended victorious Christ, in whom both Jew and Gentile become one new man. This church, this calling out was kept a secret, hid in God until it was first revealed to Paul. Its calling, standing and hope were all hidden in God as the Great Secret but has now been revealed. Interestingly, the Jews at Pentecost had received all this within the spirit of Christ, but they had no idea nor did they understand what God had given to them. It was not made known until many years later when Paul received the revelation of the Great Secret from God. In fact, in the years following Pentecost many Christian Jews were zealous of the Law and strongly resisted Paul's ministry. The Book of Acts documents much of this behaviour.

The purpose of the ages is therefore centred in Jesus Christ. He is the firstborn of many sons and all things will be made new in him. There is a future time when all things not of Christ will diminish, and all things in Christ will be in glory. God has made known to us this secret of His will:

"Having made known unto us the mystery of his will...

That in the dispensation of the fulness of times he might gather together in one all things in Christ.....

That we should be to the praise of his glory....."
(Ephesians 1:9, 10 and 12)

In Christ, we will be gathered up and presented in his glory.

Conclusion

Therefore, we must handle the Word of God carefully so that we may separate out what God has placed in each different age or administration. Then we can go on to appreciate how special this Age of Grace truly is and how unique it is. How full of splendour is the Word of God that unfolds this Great Secret, which in all other ages had been hid in God.

210

Part XI - The Walk of Power

Chapter 43: The walk of power in the Great Secret

The same spirit of Christ

Every person in the Body of Christ has received the same spirit, however, not everyone chooses to walk in the spirit in exactly the same way. This is a matter of every individual's believing what the Word of God says. Some Christians believe more of the Word than others. However, there are different outward evidences of the internal presence of the gift of holy spirit within a person.

Jesus explains

In the first century the Apostles knew that they had received power from on high when they received the gift of holy spirit. Jesus Christ had already explained this to them before Pentecost.

> "But ye shall receive power after that [*when*] the Holy Ghost is come upon you..." (Acts 1:8)

and,

> "And, behold, I send the promise of my Father upon you: but tarry ye in the city of Jerusalem, until ye be endued with power from on high." (Luke 24:49)

Here, in both Acts and Luke, the Word of God shows us that the spirit of Christ in us is also power (Gr. *dunamis*) from God. The Greek word for power here means latent power or potential power. As such, it is like the latent power that is in a car battery. It requires harnessing. It must be worked. To complete our understanding, there are other words for power in the New Testament. These are "*exousia*" which means authority (i.e. the

212

power to act) and *"energemata"* which means exercised power like kinetic energy or energy put to use (i.e. power in motion).

Powerful signs

Jesus Christ had also said that signs would follow believers so the Apostles walked in believing and expecting the words of Jesus to be fulfilled in their own lives.

"And these signs shall follow them that believe; in my name shall they cast out devils; they shall speak with new tongues.

They shall take up serpents [*devil spirits*]; and if they drink any deadly thing, it shall not hurt them; they shall lay hands on the sick, and they shall recover." (Mark 16:17-18)

We too are to walk in this same believing and expectation of God's Word, and we too shall see signs, miracles and wonders as His Word promises. Christ is in us. We too are appointed to manifest this power of the Christ in us.

The nine manifestations of holy spirit

There are nine manifestations of holy spirit. These manifestations are outward evidences of the internal power of the spirit in us. Each manifestation is given to every man and each manifestation is given for a profit:

"But the manifestation of the spirit is given to every man to profit withal.

For to one [*profit*] is given by the Spirit the word of wisdom; to another [*profit*] the word of knowledge by the same Spirit; To another [profit] faith by the same Spirit; to another [profit] the gifts of healing by the same Spirit;

To another [profit] the working of miracles; to another [profit] prophecy; to another [profit] discerning of spirits; to another [profit] *divers* kinds of tongues; to another [profit] the interpretation of tongues:

But all these worketh that one and selfsame Spirit, dividing to every man severally as he will." (1 Corinthians 12:7-11).

Gift or manifestation?

However, there is both a startling truth and a startling error that we are all surrounded with in Christendom. In all the critical Greek texts of the New Testament, the nine manifestations of holy spirit are never called "gifts of the spirit" by God. Now, I do know that man and some Bible translations have called them "gifts of the spirit" but that is man speaking not God speaking. God calls them the manifestation of holy spirit. The reason why this is so important is that God has given us the gift of holy spirit which in truth is also the latent power of all nine manifestations within us. God has not given some of us only half a spirit; neither has He given some more spirit than others but rather He has placed all nine manifestations as potential power in the same gift of holy spirit that we have all received. Now it is the Devil's will to get some of us believing that the manifestations are gifts. Nothing could be farther from the truth. The Devil does not want us to learn from God how we are to walk in these powerful evidences of the spirit of Christ in us.

Instead of simply believing what God's Word says, the Devil wants us to think that they are gifts because perhaps we will then go on to think that we haven't received some of them as they are gifts that God hands out only to a chosen few. Any Christian falling under this error is likely to be perpetuating the Devil's lie and hinder the authority that Christians have to exercise the power of the Christ in them. However, in God's will, we have been given the authority to walk in the power of the spirit.

214

Ye shall receive into manifestation

There is a record in Acts which is very enlightening regarding God's all inclusive approach to the manifestations.

"Then Peter said unto them, Repent, and be baptized every one of you in the name of Jesus Christ for the remission of sins, and ye shall receive the gift of the Holy Ghost.

For the promise is unto you, and to your children, and to all that afar off, *even* as many as the Lord our God shall call." (Acts 2:38-39)

The Greek word for receive in this verse is "*lambano*" and it means far more than just receiving the gift of holy spirit. The Greek word "*lambano*" means to receive it into manifestation. What Peter was actually saying was all those who believe on the Lord Jesus Christ shall absolutely receive the same spirit into manifestation like the Apostles had done so in Acts 2:1-4. In other words, we would all speak with tongues. God does not leave any of His children short with only half the spirit, but rather He has given us all the same measure of Christ. Later, Paul would write to the Corinthians that it was God's will for all Christians to speak in tongues and bring forth words of prophecy

"I would that ye all speak with tongues, but rather that ye prophesied..." (1 Corinthians 14:5)

God wants all the members of the Body of Christ to manifest holy spirit. The word "would" here is old English for want or desire. God desires for all members of the Body of Christ to speak in tongues because there are numerous spiritual benefits of speaking in tongues that we need in order to grow up spiritually. He has enabled us so let us learn His ways in the spirit and trust His Word to us.

When we manifest the gift of holy spirit that is in us, we are manifesting the Christ that is in us. Today, we can walk in the power of Christ and grow up into him, learning to manifest his ability which is in the spirit in us.

Part XII – The Ministers of the Great Secret

Chapter 44: Apostles, prophets, pastors and teachers of the Great Secret

Directions from God

For the most part the organised visible church today is ignorant of the Great Secret. It appears that some organisations and their leaders neither know of it nor wish to know it; neither do they wish to handle it correctly in the sight of God. In Romans 16:25-26, God declares that this Great Secret is revealed for the obedience of faith. This means that the Great Secret is exactly what Father wants us to believe. In order to be obedient in believing, Father requires that we believe and practise the Great Secret. God has also revealed that the Great Secret is the standard of administration in the household – that is how He wants the affairs of the Church to be organised. True leaders labour in this direction; false apostles, false prophets, false pastors and false teachers work against God and against His will in these regards. True apostles, true prophets, true pastors and true teachers will build up the household of the Church in the glorious riches of the Great Secret.

Qualifications to be a deacon

The Greek word for deacon in the Bible is *"diakonos"* and means minister. A deacon is someone who ministers in the Body of Christ. Apostles, prophets, pastors and teachers are ministers in the Body of Christ. A minister is also someone who takes charge of a fellowship group giving them spiritual direction and teaching.

Now God sets out in His Word the qualifications a person must have before being appointed to the position of a deacon in the

Body of Christ. One of these qualifications is the requirement to hold the knowledge of the Great Secret in a pure heart.

"Likewise *must* the deacons *be* grave, not double tongued, not given to much wine, not greedy of filthy lucre;

Holding the mystery of the faith in a pure conscience."
(1 Timothy 3:8-9)

The word "conscience" refers to the heart of a man. And the word "holding" is "*scheo*" in the Greek which means to keep a continuing strong and firm grip on something through possession and ability. In this case, the person to be appointed to the leadership position of a deacon must have a strong understanding of the secret and must have given this doctrine the pre-eminence in his heart. Therefore, a deacon must continue to hold and possess the Great Secret in his heart. This requirement is very logical because out of the heart are the issues of life. The life of the deacon is to be centred on the household administration of the Great Secret for the One Body of Christ. And so, if the deacon is holding the secret in his heart, then he is qualified to go about God's business. The Great Secret will be the issues of his life because of what is in his heart.

False leaders in today's Church

The presence of false leaders in the Church is no new thing. In the first century, there were many so called leaders who were not approved by the Father and the Lord Jesus Christ. There are many records in the Epistles that give testimony to this fact. Today, there are many false apostles, prophets, pastors and teachers who appoint themselves and there are many who are also appointed by the Devil to further his purposes.

As we have seen, our heavenly Father has said that the household administration is the Great Secret. The administration refers to how God wants His household to be governed. Therefore, to be a leader in the Church, a person must know and be obedient to the Great Secret. Can you imagine a business manager not knowing how his bosses would want the business to be managed? Or a Cabinet Minister of a worldly government who did not know the policies of his party; or a headmaster who did not know the rules of his school? How absurd! Then why are there so many so called leaders in the Church who do not know the household administration of the Great Secret? How can a prophet bring the sons of God back to God's Word if that so called prophet does not know the secret?

Paul declared to Timothy that to be a deacon, a requirement is to first hold the secret in a pure heart. In God's eyes, many who call themselves leaders today are not yet fit to lead the Church because they do not yet hold the secret in a pure heart. Many call themselves apostles, prophets, pastors and teachers and yet they do not even know that there is a secret which is the administration of God's church. True apostles and prophets have the revelation of the secret in their heart:

> "Which in other ages was not made known unto the sons of men, as it is now revealed unto his holy apostles and prophets by the Spirit" (Ephesians 3:5)

True apostles and prophets receive the revelation of the Great Secret and then faithfully make it known to others. It is time for the Church to wake up and mature into God's will. False apostles, prophets, pastors and teachers stand out clearly because they either deny the Great Secret or do not hold it in their hearts. The Church needs to send the Devil running from the greatness of the secret rather than allowing him to court the Church through weak and false leadership. The spiritual well being of God's household, the will of God and the truth are paramount.

> "My brethren, be not many masters, knowing that we shall receive the greater condemnation [*judgment*]." (James 3:1).

In Old Testament times before the Great Secret was revealed, God showed His displeasure towards the false leaders who were disobedient in fulfilling their responsibilities towards the people of God:

> "My people are destroyed for lack of knowledge: because thou hast rejected knowledge, I will also reject thee, that thou shalt be no priest to me" (Hosea 4:6a).

It is a serious matter with God today whenever members of the Body of Christ are destroyed by the Adversary through their lack of knowledge of the greatness of the secret in Christ. God does not want His children to be tossed to and fro with every wind of doctrine, but rather established in the Great Secret with all its blessings and glorious riches – this is the work and responsibility of the leaders in the Body of Christ.

The work of true and faithful leadership

God works mightily in those who labour to present believers perfect in the Great Secret in Christ:

> "To whom God would make known what *is* the riches of the glory of this mystery among the Gentiles; which is Christ in you, the hope of glory:
>
> Whom we preach, warning every man, and teaching every man in all wisdom; that we may present every man perfect in Christ Jesus:
>
> Whereunto I also labour, striving according to his working, which worketh in me mightily." (Colossians 1:27-29)

True apostles, true prophets, true pastors and true teachers strive according to His working, which works in them mightily. This is the power of God at work in his ministers. God's working is centred on the Great Secret in Christ and our growing in the secret.

Faithful stewards

True leaders in the Body of Christ are faithful stewards of the secrets of God, including the Great Secret of Christ and his Church.

> "Let a man so account of us, as of the ministers of Christ, and stewards of the mysteries of God.
>
> Moreover it is required in stewards, that a man be found faithful." (1 Corinthians 4:1-2)

Ministers of God are stewards of His Word who work among his people here on earth. They are stewards of the secrets of God. Faithful stewards are those who do not adulterate or water down the Word of their master.

The purpose of the gift ministries

God gave gift ministries to the Body of Christ as spiritual leaders:

> "And he gave some, apostles; and some, prophets; and some, evangelists; and some pastors and teachers;" (Ephesians 4:11)

The spiritual leaders in the Church are apostles, prophets, evangelists, pastors and teachers. They are appointed by God and not man. The reasons God gave these gifts of leadership to the Church are set out in the next verses:

> "For the perfecting of the saints, for the work of the ministry, for the edifying of the body of Christ:" (Ephesians 4:12)

God wants the minds of the saints to be perfected in the Great Secret. The gift ministries, who are the spiritual leaders in the Body of Christ, are to work in harmony with God to spiritually nurture the Body of Christ to grow up into Christ:

> "Till we all come in the unity of the faith, and of the knowledge of the Son of God, unto a perfect man, unto the measure of the stature of the fulness of Christ:"
> (Ephesians 4:13)

and that

> "...speaking the truth in love, may grow up into him in all things, which is the head, *even* Christ" (Ephesians 4:15)

The works of the gift ministries are centred on the Great Secret.

Conclusion

Today, the Word of God requires all leaders to be grounded in the Great Secret, even before they are appointed to leadership positions in the Church.

According to the Almighty God, anyone who does not comprehend the Great Secret and ably hold it faithfully in their heart is not ready to lead the Body of Christ and should not be in a leadership position. Yet, how many so called leaders there are who are without this spiritual qualification. They are not yet fit to lead and should humbly seek God who can establish them in the Great Secret first. And when they become grounded and settled in the secret, then they will be able to serve in the Body of Christ.

True leaders will strengthen the Body of Christ and build it up in the blessings of the Great Secret.

Chapter 45: Speaking the Great Secret boldly

We are approaching the end of the book and you will now know the Great Secret in more depth than the majority of our brothers and sisters in Christ since it was first revealed nearly two thousand years ago. Therefore, take all of the teachings in this book to heart so that you may minister effectively and powerfully in accordance with the proper household administration of God for this age in which we live. You will then be able to strengthen the Body of Christ and build it up in God's will. The more you grow up into Christ, the more you will be able to help others come into the knowledge and understanding of the Great Secret. Then, they too can begin to be perfected in Christ.

"As I ought to speak"

When you speak the Great Secret to fellow Christians, seek to speak it boldly and lovingly with inspiration from the Father. Paul wrote to the Colossians on this wise:

"Continue in prayer, and watch in the same with thanksgiving;

Withal praying also for us, that God would open unto us a door of utterance, to speak the mystery of Christ, for which I am also in bonds;

That I may make it manifest, as I ought to speak."
(Colossians 4:2-4)

Let us also pray for everyone who knows this secret that doors of utterance may be opened to us all. Every member of the Body of Christ should hear of its greatness. God wants to make it known to every Christian. You and I comprehend the breadth, length, depth and height of this Great Secret in Christ; we should always be ready to speak it boldly as it is God's will and He will lead and direct us.

"Ambassadors for the secret of the gospel"

Speaking the Great Secret boldly is how it ought to be preached. It is interesting that Paul asked the Christians in Ephesus to pray for him that inspired utterance may be given to him and that he may speak boldly to make known the secret of the gospel.

> "And for me, that utterance may be given unto me, that I may open my mouth boldly, to make known the mystery of the gospel,
>
> For which I am an ambassador in bonds: that therein I may speak boldly, as I ought to speak." (Ephesians 6:19-20)

Paul said that he was an ambassador for the secret of the gospel. You and I are also ambassadors for the secret of the gospel. God has unfolded its meaning to our hearts; therefore, our mission is now to also make known the Great Secret.

Anyone speaking the Great Secret in Christ "ought to speak" boldly as an ambassador. If you were an ambassador for one of the nations in the world, you would speak with the authority of that country. Paul was an ambassador for "the secret of the gospel" and he would speak with God's authority concerning the Great Secret. This is God's way.

Today, the Body of Christ needs ambassadors for the Great Secret to make it known among Christians. Therefore, when you speak the truth of the secret, remember that you are speaking with the authority of God Almighty. It is His household administration and we know that He reveals it for the obedience of faith. The Great Secret is the will of God.

Word over the world

Paul was a fellow labourer with God in making known the secret. Paul worked to make all men see what the household administration of the secret is. You too are a fellow labourer with God. God's heart is for every person in the world to be saved and come to the full knowledge of the Great Secret. This is what we call "Word over the world".

"For this *is* good and acceptable in the sight of God our Saviour;

Who will have all men to be saved, and to come unto the knowledge [Gr. *epignosis*] of the truth." (1 Timothy 2:3-4)

The real meaning of "Word over the world" is that the Great Secret in Christ is known and lived amongst men. It is God's vision and it is becoming our vision also.

So, we speak the Great Secret boldly. We pray for open doors that this secret may be made known. It is God who works in people's hearts as they hear this Word about the secret. As ambassadors for the secret of the gospel, we speak boldly and make it known, and God is with us. As ambassadors, we speak directly in the presence of God.

Chapter 46: Understanding the Epistles through the Great Secret

The subject matter of the Epistles of Paul is the Great Secret in Christ. Without grasping this, many of the scriptures simply cannot be understood. On the other hand, reading the Epistles in light of the knowledge of the secret will afford an understanding greater than ever before. For example, 1 Corinthians 2:10 speaks of "the deep things of God". We now understand that Paul was referring to the riches of the glory of the secret which are a key part of comprehending the "breadth, and length and depth and height" of the secret itself. The context of 1 Corinthians chapter 2 is the Great Secret. Without knowing this, and understanding what the Great Secret is all about, these scriptures simply cannot be unfolded in our understanding.

Similarly, Paul wrote to Timothy that he should charge some in the Church that only the doctrine of the Great Secret should be taught in the Body of Christ:

> "As I besought thee to abide still at Ephesus, when I went into Macedonia, that thou mightest charge some that they teach no other doctrine" (1 Timothy 1:3)

There are countless examples like these in the Epistles. When you comprehend the Great Secret, it is very interesting to see how God is continually leading His people towards the obedience to and the full understanding of the Great Secret.

The Epistles of Paul record precept upon precept of the Great Secret concerning Christ and those called out to him. When you know by experience that it is Christ in you, then you have the key to open up the true understanding of what is written in these Epistles. Only then will the Epistles come alive in your understanding. Everyone who reads them in this light will be thrilled at the manifold wisdom of God at the heart of this Great Secret.

Everything in the Epistles should be understood in the context of the Great Secret. Our heavenly Father wants us to know his will in all wisdom and spiritual understanding.

Part XIII - The Adversary and the Great Secret

Chapter 47: The turning away from the Great Secret

The shock of the Devil

It was a great shock to the Devil when he witnessed the resurrection of Christ. The Devil thought he had conquered Jesus forever by death, but he was wrong. Jesus was raised from the dead and ascended to the Father to take his place far above all principality and dominion and power, including the entire kingdom of the Adversary. The Devil saw Jesus Christ take his place at the right hand of God.

It was even more of a shock to the Devil when he witnessed the spirit of Christ dwelling in every believer from Pentecost onwards. In the spirit realm, the Adversary was now being faced with millions of believers having Christ in them. But when the first century believers started walking in the greatness of the revelation of what it really is to have Christ inside, when they began to grow up into Christ in all things and walk like him, then the Adversary received his greatest shock of all time as his entire kingdom was being undermined on a daily basis by more than tens of thousands of Christians. He was no longer faced with just one Jesus Christ working against his kingdom. Rather, he was now faced with Christ in action within every faithful Christian. The power and nature of God in Christ was being manifest in many places, and so the Devil's purposes were being brought to nothing. He had never seen such a power against him as was being manifest by the Body of Christ.

Two years and three months

There is a record in the Book of Acts about Paul's ministry which tells us how the Word of God had spread like wild fire throughout the Middle East:

> "And he went into the synagogue and spake boldly for the space of three months, disputing and persuading the things concerning the kingdom of God.
>
> But when divers were hardened, and believed not, but spake evil of that way before the multitude, he departed from them, and separated the disciples, disputing daily in the school of one Tyrannus.
>
> And this continued by the space of two years; so that all they which dwelt in Asia heard the word of the Lord Jesus, both Jews and Greeks." (Acts 19:8-10)

Within 2 years and 3 months, all of Asia Minor had heard the Word of God via the outreach ministry of the Apostle Paul. Many of those who had heard also believed and were saved. And they were being taught the Great Secret in Christ. However, the Adversary was not going to just sit back and simply let this happen.

The Devil's response: the Great Secret short-lived in their hearts

Within that short space of time, all the people in Asia Minor had heard witness of the Word of God. The Church had grown and was beginning to live the glorious secret in Christ. Yet, only a few years later, by the time 2 Timothy had been written, all they which were in Asia had turned away from the Apostle Paul:

"This thou knowest, that all they which are in Asia be turned
away from me; of whom are Phygellus and Hermogenes."
(2 Timothy 1:15)

What had happened? Well, this was the Devil's work. What this
really meant was that the believers had turned away from Paul's
gospel which, as we know, is the truth of the revelation of the
Great Secret. It had now become the Adversary's primary aim to
deal with the expansion of the truth of this Great Secret. Two of
the key strands to his strategy were to lead believers away and
then conceal the Great Secret by setting up a false Christianity.
For the most part, the Adversary was successful as Paul's
statement testifies: "all they which are in Asia be turned away
from me". They had been turned away from Paul and his gospel
which is the Great Secret. They had been turned away by the
Adversary's actions.

In response to the mighty expansion of the Great Secret among
the believers, the Devil had mustered up his devil spirits and sent
them to work to talk the believers out of their calling from God. It
was now an all out war on the Great Secret in Christ. Many
believers had been duped. Even many leaders in the first century
Church had been tricked out of continuing in the Great Secret:

"For Demas hath forsaken me, having loved this present
world, and is departed unto Thessalonica, Crescens to Galatia,
Titus unto Dalmatia." (2 Timothy 4:10)

Sadly, the majority of believers in Asia Minor had accepted the
Adversary's call rather than God's call to walk in the obedience
of faith. The Great Secret was practically lost to the majority in
Asia Minor, even in the first century. They had begun to walk by
the flesh and not by the spirit of Christ in them - they ceased from
holding the head of the One Body. They did not hold in a pure
heart the Great Secret which is the true faith of Jesus Christ.
Rather, they became corrupted with the Devil's most effective

religion of all time namely counterfeit Christianity which continues in abundance all around today.

It happened to the Galatians

Some of the details of the "turning away" from the Great Secret are recorded in the Epistle to the Galatians. This epistle records how the decay had already set into the Church and how Paul was offering to them a hand of deliverance from their error.

> "I marvel that ye are so soon removed from him that called you into the grace of Christ unto another gospel:
>
> Which is not another; but there be some that trouble you, and would pervert the gospel of Christ.
>
> But though we, or an angel from heaven, preach any other gospel unto you than that which we have preached unto you, let him be accursed." (Galatians 1:6-8)

Paul was pointing out to them that they were being led away by a perversion of the gospel of the Great Secret. He then went on to remind them that he had received the gospel of the Great Secret not from man, but by revelation from God. This is what they were being removed from. The Adversary had sent people to encourage them to walk by the flesh and not by the spirit of Christ. So Paul confronts them again:

> "O foolish Galatians, who hath bewitched you, that ye should not obey the truth, before whose eyes Jesus Christ hath been evidently set forth, crucified [*again*] among you?
>
> This only would I learn of you, Received ye the spirit by the works of the law, or by the hearing of faith?
>
> Are you so foolish? Having begun in the spirit, are ye now made perfect by the flesh?" (Galatians 3:1-3)

As we have said in an earlier chapter, the Great Secret is opened up to the new man when we walk in the spirit. But here, the Galatians had effectively trodden under foot the crucifixion of our Lord Jesus Christ because they had turned away from its true meaning. Instead of walking by the spirit and growing up into Christ, they discarded the new man and returned to walk by the flesh as if nothing had been provided for them in the Great Secret in Christ. Things in the Galatian Church had got so far removed from the true household administration of the Great Secret that Paul had to work to form Christ again in their hearts:

"My little children, of whom I travail in birth again until Christ be formed in you" (Galatians 4:19)

In the last two chapters of Galatians, Paul would remind them of the works of the flesh and the fruit of the spirit. He was highlighting that they had a choice. If they were to sow to their flesh, they would only reap corruption and destruction. But if they were to sow to the spirit, their efforts would be rewarded with fruit that would be everlasting. They had a choice about the man of their heart. He pointed them to the new creation in Christ:

"For in Christ Jesus neither circumcision availeth anything, nor uncircumcision, but a new creature.

And as many as walk according to this rule, peace *be* upon them, and mercy....." (Galatians 6:15-16)

The new man in Christ is one of the key building blocks of the Great Secret and the Galatians had dismissed it.

At the future gathering together, when we will see Jesus Christ, all things will become plain. In that day, it will be a surprise to many Christians how much of the Word of God concerning the Great Secret has been perverted and how far many have strayed from the "obedience of faith".

Today

However, in the Church today, we are faced with the same choices that the Christians in Galatia were faced with. We don't have to look very far to see that the spiritual darkness produced by the "turning away" in the first century continues all around us today in Christendom.

The "turning away" will be continued today by any Christian who walks by the flesh and not by the revealed word of God which is walking by faith. The flesh will fail to keep the unity of spirit because the flesh walk by its very nature causes divisions. This flesh walk originally gave rise to many sects and groups in the first century. It defiles the truth of the One Body of Christ. The walk of the flesh erodes the truth of what God had done for the believer in Christ and replaces it with other ideas. In the first century, grace was eventually replaced by works and the knowledge of the one new man was practically lost to most. The blessed hope of looking forward to the gathering together in Christ was eventually replaced with the uncertain looking for the judgement of God as Christians forgot what God had accomplished for them through Christ.

In the first century, the Great Secret was buried so deeply by the Adversary's actions that for the most part today, the organised visible Church is still in a state of loss regarding the Great Secret. Yet, there is no need for this to be. The organised visible Church does not have to remain as a loser to the Adversary. God's heartfelt desire is to make the Great Secret known to us all so that we will be strengthened and blessed by its riches. There is no need for any of us to hold back today.

Conclusion

The Great Secret is the very essence of and at the very centre of the faith of Jesus Christ. It is the true faith. When it was lost, all manner of counterfeit so called Christian religious ideas took its place. Simply, the "turning away" in the first century Church was a turning away from the Great Secret and from the true faith. It was devised by the Adversary. The power and love of God in growing up into Christ were replaced by man's religious teachings; and then, true Biblical understanding was lost to many.

Despite all this, many Christians today are rediscovering what was lost. You and I have discovered the lost secret of Christianity. God calls it the Great Secret. We are the faithful in Christ, and God's promises to us are truly great:

> "But we all, with open face beholding as in a glass the glory of the Lord, are changed into the same image from glory to glory, *even* as by the Spirit of the Lord." (2 Corinthians 3:18)

Therefore, we shall continue to rise up in this Great Secret going forward from glory to glory, from strength to strength, from one rich blessing to another rich blessing. As God has said, the Great Secret was appointed before the world for our glory. Yes, it is our glory indeed as we turn away from the Adversary and turn to the Word of our God to embrace the obedience of faith. Moreover, in the strength of Christ we shall turn again to the Adversary only this time it will be with the fire of the Great Secret burning in our hearts. And we shall speak of his defeat which is already in us, that greater is Christ in us than all the devils in the world put together. We will tread him under our feet as we walk all over his kingdom of this world living victoriously and manifesting the riches of the glory of the secret he so dislikes.

> "And the God of peace shall bruise Satan under your feet shortly. The grace of our Lord Jesus Christ *be* with you. Amen." (Romans 16:20)

Bruising Satan under our feet ....so be it.

Chapter 48: The end of the Adversary in the Great Secret

The end of the Adversary's reign has now begun

In this chapter, we will see how the Adversary has failed again and again throughout history and how, in the Great Secret, God deals the death blow to the Adversary's head. In the Great Secret, the world ends and the reign of the Adversary is gone. All things are made new and whatsoever is born of God has already overcome the world. He has been defeated by the Lord Jesus Christ through the wisdom of God.

Outright hostility to the Great Secret

The Adversary is out rightly hostile to the Great Secret. He hates it. His religious leaders work against it and there is no place for it as far as they are all concerned. This is because the Adversary, his devil spirits and his ministers here on earth have no place to stand in the Great Secret. They are all finished. But God appointed it for our glory and so it will be. To us it is life.

The promised seed

Since Eden, the Adversary has worked against the promised seed who is Jesus Christ. He knew that one day Jesus Christ would come because God had foretold it when He spoke directly to the Adversary in the Garden of Eden:

> "And I will put enmity between thee and the woman, and between thy seed and her seed; it shall bruise thy head, and thou shalt bruise his heel." (Genesis 3:15)

Throughout history

Throughout history, the Adversary worked to prevent this seed (i.e. Jesus Christ) appearing and saving mankind. In the days of Herod, the Adversary sought to kill all children under the age of two. His intention was to kill Jesus, the promised seed, but Joseph and Mary escaped to Egypt and he failed:

> ".... The angel of the Lord appeareth to Joseph in a dream, saying, Arise, and take the young child and his mother, and flee into Egypt, and be thou there until I bring thee word: for Herod will seek the young child to destroy him."
> (Matthew 2:13)

However, there was an appointed time when he would be allowed by God to crucify our Lord Jesus Christ. Although at the crucifixion, he naively thought he had won his long standing battle with God. But our Father raised up Jesus Christ from the dead and the wicked old Adversary failed yet again. But then it was about to get a whole lot worse for him from this point forward.

The Adversary defeated in the Great Secret

Jesus Christ ascended to the Father and the gift of holy spirit was sent at Pentecost to all those who believed on Jesus Christ. Some years after Pentecost, it was revealed what God had actually done in the gift of holy spirit. The believers had received Christ in them and they had received "the riches of the glory of the mystery" (Colossians 1:27). This Great Secret was revealed to Paul and it was unfolded in the hearts and lives of the faithful. Christ was now in every believer and the Adversary was now faced with millions of believers with Christ in them. In the spirit realm he was no longer faced with just one Jesus Christ. Rather, he was faced with millions of Christ spirits. Every believer had Christ in them. But then it was to get even worse than ever for the Adversary.

Not only was Christ in all, but the Apostle Paul and his fellow labourers were teaching the believers how to walk in this Great Secret and what it really means to have Christ in them. Christ was being formed in their hearts so that they were manifesting Christ in everything that they did and said. They were truly living the Christ in them and they were undermining the Adversary's authority as well as exposing and undoing his works on every hand.

This is why it is written that if the Adversary and his ruling devil spirits had known the Great Secret, they would not have crucified Christ:

> "But we speak the wisdom of God in a mystery, *even* the hidden *wisdom*, which God ordained before the world unto our glory:

> Which none of the princes of this world knew: for had they known *it*, they would not have crucified the Lord of glory." (1 Corinthians 2:7-8)

This secret is called "Great" by God. So great is it that the Adversary would have preferred to be faced with one Jesus Christ than the many millions who now have Christ in them. Therefore, he would not have crucified the Lord of glory. However, in His wisdom, God kept the Great Secret hid in Himself until the time came to reveal it to the Apostle Paul. This was God's plan.

The Adversary's head bruised

God had bruised Satan under the believers' feet. So Paul, knowing what was happening spiritually, would write to the believers in Rome that:

"... the God of peace shall bruise Satan under your feet shortly. The grace of our Lord Jesus Christ *be* with you all. Amen." (Romans 16:20)

A few verses later he went on to say that God has the power to establish them in the Great Secret:

"Now to him that is of power to stablish you according to my gospel and the preaching of Jesus Christ, according to the revelation of the mystery, which was kept secret since the world began" (Romans 16:25)

Paul knew that God would establish them in the one new man of the Great Secret. Everything that the adversary is and everything that he has done is under the feet of this one new man which is all Christ. This one new man is of the incorruptible seed by which we have been born again and it is also of the promised seed in Genesis that bruises the head of the serpent, the Adversary.

So, in the Great Secret, the Adversary's kingdom is being shaken at its very roots. In the Great Secret, God has undermined the Adversary spectacularly. What a story! This is one of the many aspects of the wisdom of God in the Great Secret. How rich is this Great Secret that God had kept hid in Himself until it was time to reveal it to the Apostle Paul. The greatness of the secret surpasses anything that the Adversary can do.

Chapter 49: The Adversary's work against the Great Secret

The wiles of the Devil

At this juncture, all the Adversary could do to the believers was to attempt talk the members of the Church out of what they truly are in Christ. So, as we have seen he devised a counterfeit Christianity in order to bury the Great Secret by replacing it with something else:

> "I marvel that ye are so soon removed from him that called you into the grace of Christ unto another gospel:
>
> Which is not another; but there be some that trouble you and would pervert the gospel of Christ." (Galatians 1:6-7)

Another gospel appeared which was not another as such but rather it was a perversion of the true faith. Counterfeit Christianity continues all around us today. The Adversary still wants to blind the minds of all those who do not believe. God says that if any man preaches a different gospel than the Great Secret, let that man be cursed:

> "But though we, or an angel from heaven, preach any other gospel unto you than that which we have preached unto you, let him be accursed.
> As we said before, so say I now again, If any *man* preach any other gospel unto you than that ye have received, let him be accursed." (Galatians 1:8-9)

In the Great Secret, the Church is set free. But in the Adversary's way, which is outside the obedience of faith and outside the household administration, there is only bondage and destruction.

That way is cursed. Furthermore, God says that a curse hangs over any person, Christian or non Christian, who preaches any other gospel against the truth of the Great Secret. The gravity of the words "let him be accursed" is a severe warning to all. For Christians upon whom this curse hangs, that part of their person will be destroyed by God:

> "If any man defile the temple of God, him shall God destroy; for the temple of God is holy, which *temple* ye are."
> (1 Corinthians 3:17)

God will do this in the future by fire; yet by this fire, that same Christian will be saved from his wickedness. This is the meaning of the phrase "yet so as by fire":

> "Every man's work shall be made manifest: for the day shall declare it, because it shall be revealed by fire; and the fire shall try every man's work of what sort it is.
>
> If any man's work abide which he hath built thereupon, he shall receive a reward.
>
> If any man's work shall be burned, he shall suffer loss: but he himself shall be saved; yet so as by fire."
> (1 Corinthians 3: 13-15)

As we have seen in an earlier chapter, everyone who has accepted Christ will be saved, even if some will need to be saved so as by fire. Upon some, this future destruction in the fire is the curse that Paul spoke of to the Galatians. Here in Corinthians, we learn that the man of the heart of some will be destroyed. The words "him shall God destroy" refer to the man of the heart of some upon whom the curse from God hangs and whom shall be destroyed. However, God's Word also clearly teaches that a born again believer who has become an idolater will be saved but the idolatrous man of his heart will be destroyed. This is simple. However, for all of us who have become in our hearts what

Christ is, we shall receive rewards. The man of our heart is Christ, and there are rewards awaiting us. Praise God.

False ministers

Today, the Adversary works to bury the knowledge and talk Christians out of what they are in Christ. His intention is also to blind the minds of men to the gospel of the glory of our Lord Jesus Christ.

> "In whom the god of this world hath blinded the minds of them which believe not, lest the light of the glorious gospel of Christ, who is the image of God, should shine unto them."
> (2 Corinthians 4:4)

You will meet people today whose minds have been polluted that they cannot receive the greatness of the Gospel of the glory of our Lord Jesus Christ. However, if the Adversary pollutes a Christian's mind with a perversion of the gospel, even that person can fall from grace in their hearts. This happened to the Galatians. Paul told them that they were "fallen from grace" and that "a little leaven leaveneth the whole lump" (Galatians 5:4b and 9). The leaven was the wrong doctrine that was against the gospel of the Great Secret. The Galatians were persuaded by people sent by the Adversary to walk in the flesh rather than in the Christ in them. Paul then goes on to declare to them that he labours again with them so that Christ could be formed in their hearts:

> "My little children, of whom I travail in birth again until Christ be formed in you,
>
> I desire to be present with you now, and to change my voice; for I stand in doubt of you." (Galatians 4:19-20)

Paul was not referring to receiving the spirit of Christ all over again but rather he was talking about working with them so that

Christ would be formed in the hearts, so that Christ would once again become the man of their hearts. They would have to start again to grow up into Christ in all things and cease walking by the flesh.

One of the Adversary's mechanisms in working against the Great Secret is his false ministers who are sent to the Church:

"For such *are* false apostles, deceitful workers, transforming themselves into the apostles of Christ.

And no marvel; for Satan himself is transformed into an angel of light.

Therefore *it is* no great thing if his ministers also be transformed as the ministers of righteousness; whose end shall be according to their works." (2 Corinthians 11:13-15)

The Adversary's chosen ministers are transformed as if they were the true ministers of God's household, only they would not teach the accuracy and integrity of the Great Secret. In the next chapter we will see how the Adversary was once appointed as the glorious one. In God's original creation, Lucifer was an angel of light but he fell from this position when he rebelled against God. Today, he works in false ministers against the Great Secret. Such false ministers are described as lying in wait to deceive:

"That we *henceforth* be no more children, tossed to and fro, and carried about with every wind of doctrine, by the sleight of men, *and* cunning craftiness, whereby they lie in wait to deceive" (Ephesians 4:14)

In the craftiness of the Devil, those who are sent by him lie in wait to deceive and to turn people away from the glorious secret. Such false ministers may not even know how they are being used by the Adversary. However, we know that strong systems of religious thought have been built up all around us which work against the secret. These religious thoughts are like leaven which leavens the whole lump. In other words they will destroy all those who take to heart the false doctrines.

His works are therefore designed to hinder us but we have a conquering spirit in us and we also have the accuracy and integrity of God's Word in us also. So, we resist him as the Word says and he will flee from us.

> "Submit yourselves therefore to God. Resist the devil, and he will flee from you." (James 4:7)

There is no place for him in the Great Secret and we give him no foothold in our hearts to talk us out of the truths of the Great Secret. He has already lost again and again and so he continues today. He is under our feet being bruised by every step we take in the Word of the Great Secret.

We wrestle against principalities

The Word of God says that greater is he that is in you than he that is in the world.

> "Ye are of God, little children, and have overcome them: because greater is he that is in you, than he that is in the world." (1 John 4:4)

The Adversary only gets by through unlawfulness and by those who allow him to work. However, we rejoice that whatsoever is born of God has already overcome the world and more accurately, overcome the Devil and his entire host.

> "For whatsoever is born of God overcometh the world: and this is the victory that overcometh the world, *even* our faith." (1 John 5:4)

The Christ in you has been born of God. Our faith overcomes the world as we believe the faith of Jesus Christ.

Conclusion

The secret is so great that the Adversary would not have crucified Jesus Christ had he known God's plans beforehand. This is very significant and shows the magnitude of the secret and how far reaching it really is. It's amazing really how that the Devil sees the Great Secret and its significance and how he understands it is a threat to him, yet few Christians today really have this knowledge or even want to know or appreciate the magnitude of this secret. In this it appears that the Church can be easily fooled yet the Adversary knows. Nevertheless, we are a thorn in the side of the Adversary. In truth, in the Great Secret, we represent his worst nightmare. We have overcome him. We are more than super conquerors because of God's work in us through the unfolding of the Great Secret in our lives. We have something in which he has no part.

The Word of God says that we have overcome the Devil and his entire host because we have been born of God. Everything in the new man is stronger and higher than the Adversary. The new man has already conquered him because we have the perfect spirit of Christ in us. In this spirit, it is impossible to sin. The Adversary has no legal rights over the new man. He is under our feet and he is being bruised daily by the God in Christ who is at work in us. We are the thorn in the Adversary's side.

Chapter 50: The bright and morning star

The morning star

There is another startling revelation in God's Word. In the beginning, Lucifer (the Devil) was created as a spirit being and was second in command to God. He had a beauty and a shining that was surpassed by none of God's created angels. It was said of Lucifer that he was:

> ".. full of wisdom, and perfect in beauty.

> Thou hast been in Eden the garden of God; every precious stone *was* thy covering.......

> Thou *art* the anointed cherub that covereth; and I have set thee *so*: thou wast upon the holy mountain of God....

> Thou *wast* perfect in thy ways from the day that thou wast created, till iniquity was found in thee.

> ..... And thou hast sinned: therefore I will cast thee as profane out of the mountain of God: and I will destroy thee, O covering cherub, from the midst of the stones of fire.

> Thine heart was lifted up because of thy beauty, thou has corrupted thy wisdom by reason of thy brightness: I will cast thee to the ground, I will lay thee before kings, that they may behold thee." (Ezekiel 28:12-17)

The words "O covering cherub" refer to the unique position that Lucifer was appointed in relation to God. He was appointed as second in command to God and he had a beauty and a brightness that surpassed all other spirits to the extent that he was called the "morning star". He was a leading light in God's creation.

"O Lucifer, son of the morning" (Isaiah 14:12b)

The literal translation of this verse is "O Lucifer, O Morning Star". In Corinthians, Paul shows us that the Adversary was an angel of light. Originally, Lucifer was a leading light to all of the other angels (spirits) that God had created. The morning star is the first light of the day that guides God's creation on behalf of God Himself. Today, Satan uses this nature and experience given to him to transform himself into an angel of light.

"And no marvel; for Satan himself is transformed into an angel of light." (2 Corinthians 11:14)

So, the adversary was originally second to God and the beauty of his shining surpassed all others. These two aspects of the Adversary's special position in God's original creation are significant in our understanding the Great Secret. Jesus Christ was to replace him as second in command to God. Jesus Christ would also become the bright and morning star to the whole of God's creation.

Jesus Christ is now the leading light not only to all mankind but also to the entire creation. However, in the Great Secret, we are the Body of Christ and we are joint heirs with Christ. The future of the Body of Christ is to rule with Christ as second in command to God. Not only will we sit with Christ judging the world, we shall also judge angels and the entire spirit world.

"Do ye not know that the saints shall judge the world? And if the world shall be judged by you, are ye unworthy to judge the smallest matters?

Know ye not that we shall judge angels? ..." (1 Corinthians 6:2-3)

The day star

Today, you and I are already becoming what Christ is. The Word of God declares that he is the day star and that he is already arising in our hearts:

> "We have also a more sure word of prophecy; whereunto ye do well that ye take heed, as unto a light that shineth in a dark place, until the day dawn, and the day star arise in your hearts" (2 Peter 1:19)

The daystar is Jesus Christ. This day star arises in your heart when you grow up into Christ in all things. This is what Peter was referring to. When we have grown up into the head which is Christ, then we will be able to see spiritually by ourselves for we will have the perfect mind of Christ.

The bright and morning star

In the book of Revelation, Jesus Christ is revealed as the bright and morning star.

> "......... I am the root and the offspring of David, *and* the bright and morning star." (Revelation 22:16b).

This shining is given to all who overcome:

> "And he that overcometh, and keepeth my works until the end, to him will I give power over the nations:
>
> And he shall rule them with a rod of iron; as the vessels of a potter shall they be broken to shivers: even as I received of my Father.
>
> And I will give him the morning star." (Revelation 2:26-28)

The bright and morning star is the same as the day star that Peter speaks of. Jesus Christ is the light of this world. The light of this star has already been given to us in the spirit of Christ in us. And this light shines in us today as Christ becomes the man of our hearts.

Chapter 51: The Word of God written in the stars

The Word of God written in the stars

God created the heavens and the earth, and He set all things in order. Part of this order is the stars and what God intended for them to mean. In the Old Testament, God reveals that He recorded His Word in the constellations of the stars. In fact, the written Word only became available during Moses' time; however, before that time the Patriarchs would read the stars in the heavens. Genesis 1:14 is one of the texts that speak of these things:

> "And God said, Let there be lights in the firmament of the heaven to divide the day from the night; and let them be for signs, and for seasons, and for days, and years" (Genesis 1:14)

The words "for signs" in the Hebrew mean to show things to come. There is an ancient knowledge which unlocked the constellations of the stars to show the Word of God. Most of this ancient knowledge is not known today and the Devil in his usual style has counterfeited this knowledge with astrology, which has nothing whatsoever to do with the Word of God. However, the ancient knowledge of the stars glorified God. Psalm 19 is very telling of this ancient knowledge. The first part of this Psalm speaks of the Word of God written in the stars whilst the second part of the Psalm speaks of the Word written in the scrolls.

> "The heavens declare the glory of God; and the firmament sheweth his handywork.
>
> Day unto day uttereth speech, and night unto night sheweth knowledge.

251

There is no speech nor language *where* their voice is not heard.

Their line is gone out through all the earth, and their words to the end of the world. In them hath he set a tabernacle for the sun" (Psalm 19:1-4).

and,

"The law of the Lord *is* perfect, converting the soul: the testimony of the Lord *is* sure, making wise the simple.

The statutes of the Lord *are* right, rejoicing the heart: the commandment of the Lord *is* pure, enlightening the eyes." (Psalm 19:7-8)

It is interesting that the Word of God was available in the period before the written Word came. The birth of Jesus Christ was written in the constellations of the stars. His death and resurrection are there. The Adversary's defeat is there. The promised seed, the atoning work of the Christ, the wounding of the serpent, the Dragon being cast from heaven, the wrath of God, the rule of the Redeemer and the Devil destroyed are all there. The major themes of the Word are written in the stars, except for one: the Great Secret cannot be found there as it was hid in God and not revealed until the appointed time when God would reveal it to Paul. Before the written Word became available, such as in the times of the Patriarchs (Abraham, Melchisidek, Noah etc), men would read the heavens.

It is interesting how the Adversary today has counterfeited the spiritual significance of the stars. Today, mention the stars and people immediately think of astrology which indeed is devil practice. Despite this, when God made the stars, He set them in the heavens as signs of future things.

The stars today – we are the shining lights of the Great Secret

We have seen that before Moses, the Word of God was written in the stars. After Moses, it was written in the scrolls. However, today, in the Great Secret, the Word of God is written in our hearts by God. The Bible says that we are living Epistles.

> "*Forasmuch as ye are* manifestly declared to be the epistle of Christ ministered by us, written not with ink, but with the spirit of the living God; not in tables of stone, but in fleshy tables of the heart." (2 Corinthians 3:3)

The Word of God is written in us. The Word of God, except the Great Secret, is written in the stars. But as far as the Great Secret is concerned we are "the stars", the guiding lights, because God has written the Word of the Great Secret in us. We are now the stars which shine as lights in the world. In Abraham's time, the stars showed forth the Word of God; today, we show forth the Word of the Great Secret:

> "That ye may be blameless and harmless, the sons of God, without rebuke, in the midst of a crooked and perverse nation, among whom ye shine as lights in the world;
>
> Holding forth the word of life ...." (Philippians 2:15-16)

The word of God says that we are living epistles known and read of men:

> "Ye are our epistle written in our hearts, known and read of all men" (2 Corinthians 3:2)

God's wisdom

The word of God says that we are seated with Christ in the heavenlies.

"And hath raised *us* up together, and made *us* sit together in heavenly *places* in Christ Jesus" (Ephesians 2:6)

Today, the many aspects of God's wisdom in the secret is being made known by us in the heavenly realm:

"To the intent that now unto the principalities and powers in heavenly *places* might be known by the church the manifold wisdom of God" (Ephesians 3:10)

In particular, the devil spirits who hold principalities and powers in the heavenlies are looking into the unfolding of the Great Secret in the lives of the called out ones, the Church. God is at work in us. The greatness of the secret is being made known by us in the heavens.

The jealousy

Jesus Christ is both the promised seed and the bright and morning star. He has replaced the Adversary as second in command to God. The glory of God is reflected in Christ, and through the Great Secret we are becoming what Christ is. Therefore, we have been born from above through the promised seed, which is also called the incorruptible seed of Christ. Spiritually, in the new birth, God has placed the Adversary under our feet. We are the Body of Christ standing above the Adversary. God is bruising Satan under our feet today as we live this Great Secret. When we grow into Christ, the day star, which is the light of Christ, arises in our hearts and we too become what Christ is, the bright and morning star. In all of this the Adversary is consumed with jealousy and envy towards all those who shine with this glory and light of Jesus Christ.

Christ has now taken the place which originally belonged to Lucifer and we are now in Christ at the very right hand of God growing into the day star and the glory of Jesus Christ. We are the lights in this world showing forth the many aspects of God's wisdom through the Great Secret.

256

Part XIV - Guarding the Great Secret

Chapter 52: Guarding the Great Secret and receiving the crown of righteousness

Guarding the faith

In 2 Timothy, Paul speaks of being near the end of his natural life. He says that he has finished his course and he has kept the faith. He made these comments referring to his work in the Great Secret.

> "For I am now ready to be offered, and the time of my departure is at hand.
> I have fought a good fight, I have finished *my* course, I have kept the faith" (2 Timothy 4:7)

Paul had completed the work given to him by God. The administration ("*oikonomia*") of the Great Secret had been entrusted to Paul and he had been commanded by God to write it down in the scriptures and make it known to the nations. Thus he would say that "I have finished my course" - Paul had completed the work that God had set for him. Then, interestingly, Paul said that he had "kept the faith". The word "faith" here refers to the true faith of Jesus Christ which is the Great Secret. The word "kept" in the Greek is "*tereo*" which is from "*tereos*" meaning to watch and guard from injury or loss. Paul was telling Timothy that he had completed the job that God had given him in making known the Great Secret and that he had guarded the Great Secret from injury or loss.

The crown of righteousness

Every member of the Body of Christ who guards the secret from injury or loss continues in the faith and becomes grounded and settled and not moved away from the hope of the gospel. On account of this such a person will also love the return of our Lord Jesus Christ. This is because the hope of his calling in the Great Secret is that we will be fully fashioned into the head, even into Christ. In that day we will be made fully like him. This is what awaits us at the return.

> "If ye continue in the faith grounded and settled, and *be* not moved away from the hope of the gospel, which ye have heard ..." (Colossians 1:23)

To everyone who guards the secret in this fashion, there will be given a special reward at the return of our Lord Jesus Christ:

> " .... I have kept [*guarded*] the faith:

> Henceforth, there is laid up for me a crown of righteousness, which the Lord, the righteous judge, shall give me at that day: and not to me only, but unto all them also that love his appearing." (2 Timothy 4:7-8)

Every Christian who guards the secret will receive the crown of righteousness. The word "crown" here refers to the garland that the winners of the Olympic Games would receive in Paul's day. Today, it is like receiving the gold medal. In total, there are five different crowns spoken of in the Epistles as rewards for believers. These crowns are for those who excel in certain areas of Christian service. They are God's rewards to the faithful. They are for the highest form of achievement in Christian service. One of these crowns is the "crown of righteousness" which awaits all those who have guarded the true faith which is the Great Secret.

In the next few chapters we shall look further into guarding the Great Secret and the instruction in God's Word on how we are to do this.

Chapter 53: Guarding the Great Secret and the unity of the spirit

Guarding the unity of the spirit

Man cannot properly guard the Great Secret without guarding the unity of the Spirit. This means guarding the spiritual unity that God has made. All members of the Body of Christ have been spiritually unified by the work of our Father in the Great Secret. In this God has done one work in all of us and this stands far above all that man can do by his own works.

> "Endeavouring to keep [Gr. "*tereo*" *meaning to guard*] the unity of the Spirit in the bond of peace." (Ephesians 4:3)

The word "unity" here is "*henotes*" which literally means the oneness. God has brought us all into the oneness. The Word of God does not say that we are to make the oneness but rather we are to guard this oneness that God has already made. There is a vast difference between the two. Making a oneness is man's will; keeping the oneness that God has made is God's will.

The oneness of the Great Secret

Father then instructs Paul to list the oneness of the Great Secret, so that we are fully instructed:

> "*There is* one body, and one spirit, even as ye are called in one hope of your calling;
> One lord, one faith, one baptism,
> One God and Father of all, who *is* above all, and through all, and in you all." (Ephesians 4:4-6)

Whenever man makes the One Body of Christ into two or more, he is not guarding the oneness that God has made and thereby he

260

is not guarding the secret. Likewise, every doctrinal departure from the faith or the Great Secret is also failing to guard the oneness and failing to guard the secret in the process. Therefore, to guard the secret, we must first recognize the oneness that God has made in all its aspects. Then, we need to ensure that our thinking and our actions are in alignment with this oneness and we do not detract from it. There are more than four thousand different denominations in Christendom, but we know that there is only One Body and one faith. There is only one Great Secret.

Guarding the secret by coming into the unity of the faith

As we have seen, God has unified us all in His setting up the Great Secret. Now it is up to us all to walk in the obedience of faith. One of the declared purposes of the gift ministries in the Word of God (apostles, prophets, pastors and teachers) is to work towards all Christians coming into the unity of the faith.

> "Till we all come in the unity of the faith, and of the knowledge of the Son of God, unto a perfect man, unto the measure of the stature of the fulness of Christ:
>
> That we *henceforth* be no more children........."
> (Ephesians 4:13-14a)

Every Christian who comes into the unity of the faith is guarding the Great Secret. The work of the gift ministries focuses on us coming to know by experience exactly who the Son of God truly is. God's will in the Great Secret is that we are all brought through the experiential knowledge of the perfect man, who is Christ. This is the one new man in which Christ is all and in all. As we look at Christ through the new man, the Bible says it is like us looking through a mirror and we are changed into the same fulness from one glory to another. We lay hold on that for which Jesus Christ has laid hold on us. This is the true one knowledge of the Son of God.

261

Hearts knit together in the Great Secret

Our Father's will is that we all come into the unity of the faith through knowing by experience the Great Secret of the one new man. At this point He knits our hearts together and we are to be comforted together. We are also to have all the riches that come by properly understanding the Secret.

> "That their hearts might be comforted, being knit together in love, and unto all riches of the full assurance of understanding, to the acknowledgement [Gr. *epignosis*] of the mystery [Gr. *musterion*] of God, and of the Father, and of Christ" (Colossians 2:2).

In harmony and unity, we shall come into the full experiential knowledge of the Great Secret. In these ways, we shall guard the Great Secret in the unity of the faith.

Chapter 54: Guarding the Great Secret by holding the head

Guarding the Great Secret by walking spiritually

There are a number of other ways by which the secret is to be guarded. One of these ways is to walk spiritually in meekness before God and in humbleness of mind before every member of the Body of Christ.

> "I therefore, the prisoner of the Lord, beseech you that ye walk worthy of the vocation wherewith ye are called,
>
> With all lowliness and meekness, with longsuffering, forbearing one another in love" (Ephesians 4:1-2)

This is the walk of the new man. The old nature will cause strife, divisions, and heresies thereby defiling and tearing down the temple of God. The new nature upholds the integrity of God's Word and protects and edifies the Body of Christ. This can only be done when what is supplied is in alignment with the Word of God. Therefore, each step that we take should be a step in the Word of God.

The head supplies

Jesus Christ is the head of the One Body. The Body of Christ functions properly when the members allow the head to supply rather than other sources such as private interpretation of the Scriptures, or man's own religious ideas or anything else that is not Christ:

> "Let no man beguile you of your reward in a voluntary humility and worshipping of angels, intruding into those

things which he hath not seen, vainly puffed up by his fleshly mind,

And not holding the Head from which all the body by joints and bands having nourishment ministered, and knit together, increaseth with the increase of God." (Colossians 2:18-19)

The nourishment comes from the head and the being knit together is a result of the members holding the head. Then, the members will grow together with the increase that comes from God. The members will grow up into the head and in so doing we all grow and increase as a temple for God:

"In whom all the building fitly framed together groweth unto an holy temple in the Lord:

In whom ye also are builded together for an habitation of God through the Spirit." (Ephesians 2:21-22)

All the members are to grow up into the head. The instruction for this growing is available today in the Epistles. The more we grow up into the head, the more effectively we can minister to the Body of Christ, to nourish it and strengthen it so that others may grow in the same way. Then, their effectiveness in building up the Body of Christ will multiply also.

What does holding the head mean?

Holding the head means holding fast to the head of the One Body of Christ. The Lord Jesus Christ is the head of the One Body. The word holding in the Greek is the word "*krateo*" which means to retain, to lay hold on, and to hold fast. This is from the root word "*kratos*" which means power, strength, might, and dominion. Interestingly, holding fast to the head will lead us all to strength. Not holding the head will lead us to us weakness. However, the meaning of the word here is to strongly lay hold on or with great vigour hold fast to something. With such strength, we shall hold fast to the head of the One Body, which is Christ.

How do we hold fast to the head?

The head of the One Body is in heaven at the right hand of God. We hold fast to the head by setting our affection on things above. Jesus Christ said that wherever our treasure is, there will be our heart also. If we treasure the spiritual things of the Great Secret, then our heart will contain the same things also and we will hold onto the head. We will develop a spiritual mind which will enable us to walk spiritually not carnally.

> "If ye then be risen with Christ, seek those things which are above, where Christ sitteth on the right hand of God.
>
> Set your affection on things above, not on things on the earth." (Colossians 3:1-2)

Our affection should be set on every word that is written to the Church in the Epistles. Holding the head is walking in the spirit which is adhering to the revelation of the written or spoken Word of God. The opposite of holding the head is walking either in the flesh or by another spirit which is not from God.

Our choice is to hold the head in One Body or to let go and enjoin the many bodies of Christendom. God beseeches us that we put forward a great effort to guard the unity that God has made in the One Body. We are not to try and make one up; God has already done the making; we are to do the keeping.

Not holding the head

Paul wrote his first letter to the Corinthians reproving them for not adhering to the truths of the One Body of Christ. The Christians at Corinth were so taken up with carnal matters that they were not holding the head. They failed to recognise one of the basic tenets of the Great Secret which is the One Body in Christ. They were eager to divide up the Body of Christ:

"For while one saith, I am of Paul; and another, I *am* of Apollos; are ye not carnal?" (1 Corinthians 3:4)

The Corinthians were intent on setting up at least two bodies of Christ! They had failed to hold onto the head and they had failed in guarding the unity that God had made.

Weak and beggarly elements

There are numerous examples of others in the Bible who failed to hold the head. In addition to the Corinthians, the Galatians did not hold the head, but rather walked by the flesh. There are also individuals mentioned in the Epistles who failed to hold the head such as Euodias and Synteche. In Christ or rather on account of the Great Secret, the believer is set free from all religious and carnal entanglements in order to embrace the freedom and the riches of the Christ in us. However, the Galatians after beginning to embrace the Great Secret were duped into seeking after other things:

"But now, after that ye have known God, or rather are known of God, how turn ye again to the weak and beggarly elements, whereunto ye desire again to be in bondage?

Ye observe days, and months, and times, and years.

I am afraid of you, lest I have bestowed upon you labour in vain." (Galatians 4:9-11)

The Galatians had become entangled with man's religious thinking and not recognised the perfect work of God in the Great Secret. Rather than walk by the spirit and by what God provides through the head, they sought fleshly things. This is not God's will for the Church for we have been set free from the weak and beggarly elements. In the new man, there is no place for the weak and beggarly elements for in the new man all things are Christ and Christ alone.

Increasing with the increase of God

Holding the head leads to receiving the increase of God.

> "And not holding the Head, from which all the body by joints and bands having nourishment ministered, and knit together, increaseth with the increase of God." (Colossians 2:19)

The increase here does not refer to the numerical increase of the church by winning souls for Christ. Rather, it refers to the spiritual increase in you and I growing up in Christ. This is true edification. It is the increase in our hearts when we are changed into the same image of Christ from glory to glory.

> "…….. which is the head, *even* Christ:
>
> From whom the whole body fitly joined together and compacted by that which every joint supplieth, according to the effectual working in every part, maketh increaseth of the body unto the edifying of itself in love." (Ephesians 4:15b-16)

Your physical head directs your physical body. Jesus Christ is the head of the One Body which is the temple of God. Our Father God is the head of Jesus Christ. The phrase "every joint supplieth" refers to God working in Christ in each member of the Body of Christ. God has placed each member of the Body of Christ as it has pleased Him. Peter says that as every man has received the gift of spirit, so we are to minister via the spirit to each other.

> "As every man hath received the gift, *even so* minister the same one to another as good stewards of the manifold grace of God." (1 Peter 4:10)

We are also to walk in the works that God has already foreordained for us.

> "For we are His workmanship created in Christ Jesus unto good works, which God hath before ordained that we should walk in them." (Ephesians 2:10)

Holding the head is being faithful. It is the same as abiding in him.

There are two ways to walk. One is right and the other is wrong.

> "Brethren, be followers together of me, and mark them which walk so as ye have us for an ensample.
>
> (For many walk, of whom I have told you often, and now tell you even weeping, *that they are* the enemies of the cross of Christ:
>
> Whose end is destruction, whose god *is their* belly, and *whose* glory *is* in their shame, who mind earthly things."
> (Philippians 3:17-19)

God tells us that any Christian who is not walking by the spirit but rather is walking carnally (in any respect) is not holding the head. This is God's specific phrase for those who are born from above but who are not faithful to walk with the spirit that God gave but rather are walking according to the deceitfulness of the flesh. Sadly, there are many Christians today who are slaves to the carnal things of the flesh, the old man nature. However, there are also many who do hold fast to the head, who are themselves an example of how to walk in the Great Secret of Christ.

In the Old Testament, God would say that the unfaithful were backsliding. In this Age of Grace, the unfaithful do not hold the head.

Part XV - The Love of God and the Great Secret

Chapter 55: The Great Secret in the love of God

The love of God is at the very heart of the Great Secret. All of the riches of the Great Secret were provided by God for us out of love. God loved us with a great love.

> "But God, who is rich in mercy, for his great love wherewith he loved us" (Ephesians 2:4)

There is much to understand regarding the love of God in relation to the Great Secret.

Before Him in love

Our Father's vision for his children is that we would live in love directly in His presence. Even before the foundation or overthrow of this world God had chosen us in Christ that we should be holy and without blame before Him in love.

> "According as He hath chosen us in him before the foundation of the world, that we should be holy and without blame before him in love" (Ephesians 1:4)

The new man, whom God created in true righteous and holiness, is seated at the right hand of God. Now it is our Father's desire that we should put on this new man in our hearts. Paul prayed for the Christians in Thessalonica that God would direct their hearts into the love of God and that they would increase and abound in this to the end that God would establish their hearts unblameable without rebuke before Him.

> "And the Lord make you to increase and abound in love one toward another, and toward all *men*, even as we *do* toward you:

To the end that he may establish your hearts unblameable
in holiness before God, even our Father, at the coming of
our Lord Jesus Christ with all his saints."
(1 Thessalonians 3:12-13).

Here, Paul is talking about the heart. The new man in us is perfect, without blame and unreproveable. However, God's purpose in this Age of Grace is that the new man dwells in our hearts; that the new man is not just in us by spirit but actually becomes the man of our heart. In order for this to happen, we must be firmly established in the love of God. Only then, can God's intention be properly fulfilled. His intention is more than placing Christ in us. Rather, He wants to see the Christ in us also dwell in our hearts.

Rooted and grounded in love and the fulness of God

In order for us to take hold of the Great Secret to the point of comprehending it, we must first be rooted and grounded in love:

"That Christ may dwell in your hearts by faith; that ye, being
rooted and grounded in love,

May be able to comprehend with all saints what *is* the breadth,
and length, and depth, and height [*of the Great Secret*]

And to know the love of Christ, which passeth knowledge,
that ye might be filled with all the fulness of God."
(Ephesians 3:17-19)

Without being rooted and grounded in love, it is impossible to truly comprehend the Great Secret. It is certainly possible to know that it is Christ in you and that there is One Body. However, to truly comprehend the breadth, length, depth and height of the secret, we must first be rooted and grounded in the love of God. When we know by experience the love of God which even goes beyond knowledge, our hearts can then be filled with the fulness of God. This fulness refers to the completeness of Christ.

The gift of the spirit of love

It is remarkable that the spirit that came at Pentecost is a spirit of love. The gift of holy spirit is the spirit of God's love. I believe that we need to see this bigger than we have ever seen it to date. Paul explains this to Timothy:

> "For God hath not given us the spirit of fear; but of power, of love, and of a sound mind." (2 Timothy 1:7)

Therefore, we ought to remember that this spirit is not just of power but also of love which is even greater. In this spirit, there is both the ability to love God our Father and to love man like He loves.

> "Beloved, let us love one another: for love is of God; and every one that loveth is born of God, and knoweth God." (1 John 4:7)

Everyone who has received the gift of holy spirit can love in this way. It is impossible for man to love this way without receiving this spirit of love first from God.

Living the truth in love may grow up into him

In order to grow up into Christ, who is the head of the One Body, we must live and speak the truth in love. In the following verse, the Greek word for "speaking" is "*athleo*" which means the entire scope of living.

> "But speaking the truth in love, may grow up into him in all things, which is the head, *even* Christ" (Ephesians 4:15)

Living the truth in love includes speaking the truth in love. By doing these things in the love of God, we will then grow up into

Christ in our hearts. This is at the very heart of God's will for us regarding the Great Secret.

Walk in love

The Epistle to the Ephesians is so rich and lofty. This is not surprising when we realise that the doctrine of the Great Secret is so beautifully unfolded in this Epistle like no other book in the Bible. Its language is befitting for the Great Secret that God had kept hid in Himself. In this Epistle we learn many things, but one of the heights is that we are imitators of God himself.

> "Be ye therefore followers of God, as dear children;
> And walk in love, as Christ hath given himself for us as an
> offering and a sacrifice to God for a sweet smelling savour."
> (Ephesians 5:1-2)

On account of the Great Secret, we have the most blessed privilege to be like our heavenly Father: to move like He moves; to speak like He speaks; to love like He loves. The word "followers" means imitators or someone who copies. As imitators of God we walk in love as Christ has also loved us.

The faith which is worked by love

The Great Secret comes to fruition in our lives through love:

> "For in Jesus Christ neither circumcision availeth anything,
> nor uncircumcision; but faith which worketh by love."
> (Galatians 5:6)

God provided the Great Secret in love. Jesus Christ walked in loving obedience to allow God to make it available to us. Today, Jesus Christ operates in love as the head of the One Body. The true faith or believing concerning Jesus Christ is brought to fruition in love. The love of God is at the heart of the

Great Secret wherever you look. Without love, there would be no Great Secret.

The final point is love

The purpose of the Word of God in the Great Secret is to bring us all into perfect love and for us to become this perfect love.

> "Now the end of the commandment is charity out of a pure heart, and *of* a good conscience, and *of* faith unfeigned" (1 Timothy 1:5)

The word "charity" is "*agape*" in the Greek which means the love of God. Our Father sees the finishing post in the race of faith where we love God and each other with the love of God arising out of three things: a pure heart; a conscience that God calls "good"; and a pure true believing concerning the perfect man, the head of the One Body which is one new man in Christ.

Part XVI – Conclusion

Chapter 56: Summary

The Greek word *"musterion"* is translated mystery in the Bible. Its real meaning is 'sacred secret' and refers to a secret knowledge that is revealed to the initiated. However, there are many secrets in the Bible but there is a special secret that God has ordained for the spiritually mature in Christ. God calls this sacred secret "the Great Secret". It is the most wonderful revelation of all time. The Church Epistles unfold this secret.

It refers to Christ and those called out to become the one new man in him. The calling, the standing and the hope of this One Body had all been kept hidden in God until He first revealed it to the Apostle Paul. It was given to Paul as the true administration of the Church for this Age in which we live. It is described in the Bible as the final piece of the jigsaw which completes the Word of God for man:

"...........to fulfil the word of God." (Colossians 1:25)

The word 'fulfil' here is the Greek word *'pleroo'* which means to fill to capacity. In other words, the Great Secret completes the Word of God i.e. fills up to capacity the Word of God. Every other subject matter had been revealed in either the Old Testament or the Gospels. Even the subject of the Book of Revelation had been revealed before. The Great Secret however cannot be found in the Old Testament because it was hidden in God during that time. However, God was to reveal it to the Apostle Paul and He commanded Paul to write it down in the Epistles which we have in our possession today. This secret would now complete the entire revelation of the Word of God to man before the return of Jesus Christ.

God declared that all of the Church's activities are to be based on this secret as it is the standard for the administration of God's household. He also commanded that the Great Secret be made known to all nations for the obedience of faith.

In the Great Secret, all the members of the One Body grow up into the head of that Body which is Christ. Today, we have been blessed with the glorious riches of Christ in us. We have died to ourselves and we are now becoming all of what Christ is.

This secret is so great that if the Devil and his ruling devil spirits had known it, they would not have crucified the Lord Jesus Christ. In God's eyes, the secret is so great that He has declared that He will destroy anyone who corrupts it.

God's heart is to make it known. He commanded the Apostle Paul to write the Great Secret in the Epistles to the churches. God wants us to comprehend the breadth, length, depth and height of the secret and to know what the riches of the glory of the secret are.

We have been created as a new man in Christ. We are neither Jew nor Gentile, but members of the One Body of Christ. We have been born from above as a spirit person which is God's own workmanship. We have been blessed with every spiritual blessing available in Christ. All of the great blessings in the Epistles are addressed to the new man of the One Body of Christ, which we are.

The heart of the Great Secret is that we grow up into Christ to be conformed to the image of Christ who is the very image of God and the express image of His glory. We are to put on the new man and we do this in our hearts. The man of our heart is to be Christ. This is God's wisdom, for He knows that out of the heart are the issues of life. The issues of our lives are to be those of Christ and the Father. We are to walk like Jesus Christ and each step we take in God's rightly divided Word we are growing up into him. We are being changed into him and are becoming more glorious each day. This is the work of our Father as He nurtures us. We are His sons by spiritual birth. One day, we will be fully like Christ. Then, the Great Secret will be finished.

God's standard for leadership is the Great Secret. He requires that all leaders in the Church hold the secret in a pure heart and that they teach this doctrine as the will of God for the Church. To this end, some leaders are to be charged that they teach no other doctrine. Rather, the leaders are to build up the members of the One Body of Christ in the strength and glory of this secret before God. Leaders should be an example in holding the head and guarding the unity of the One Body.

We know that the Great Secret has been appointed for our glory. God has declared that we will share in the Gospel of the glory of our Lord Jesus Christ and that we are joint heirs with him. We look forward to the hope of glory because it is Christ in us, the hope of his glory.

How rich in blessings are those who belong to the One Body of Christ. We live Christ and we make known the sweet essence of his knowledge in every place where we walk.

How great is the sacred secret of Christ and his called out ones? It is the greatest secret in the world today. Such is the greatness of this secret. Let us thank our heavenly Father for we now know the Great Secret. We have been initiated into this Great Secret.

Acknowledgements

The first person to introduce the Great Secret to me was Doug Baldwin. I was in my twenties and was visiting Scotland where I had previously lived for five years. I met Doug and he showed me from Colossians 1:27 that it was "Christ in me". This was to be a great turning point in my life. Since that time, many other wonderful people followed Doug in helping me to grow spiritually and to understand the Word of God in its true light and integrity. To all those people I am eternally thankful. I will be smiling when our Father gives you all your rewards.

Special thanks also go to Marjorie Conroy who lovingly under shepherded me in my early years until I could stand and walk with God by myself. Marjorie spent many hours of her time with me and taught me many things. She laid the foundation for me to grow to become a leader in the Body of Christ.

Today, I thank all my close friends in our sweet fellowship in London, England. Without their help and encouragement, it would not have been possible to write this book. In fact, the book first started many years ago as a series of teachings that I presented to the fellowship meetings in our home on Tuesday evenings. I then reworked it and presented it a second time a few years later. Then, after much further reworking and another few years, I presented it a third time at which point it metamorphosed into this book.

Ian Valentine, my brother in Christ, has been a tower of strength to me, greatly encouraging me in this work. Ian has been a faithful and consistent helper and has joined me in seeing that the Church's greatest need today is faithfulness to the household administration of the Great Secret. Ray Pereira has also been a great encouragement to me. He has grown to become an example of what it is to be a living epistle of the Great Secret.

To everyone else, including my faithful fellow labourers James Atkinson, Dave Derry, Vanessa Celerse, Debbie Bernstein, Eva Pereira, and many others too numerous to mention: I thank you all for your faithfulness, your support and especially for your walk in the Great Secret. I also thank my dear and loving wife Georgina who is a virtuous woman of God and who is my faithful spiritual helpmate in the presence of our Father. To all my brothers and sisters in Christ at our fellowship, you have enabled me to teach this Great Secret, and it is my prayer that this Word will be sounded out all over the world from all of us who come to know this Great Secret in Christ.

Special thanks also go to Ian and Nicola Valentine who did a terrific job in formatting the book and getting it ready for the printers. Thanks also go to Dave Derry and Ray Pereira both of whom designed and produced the front cover.

Lastly, and most of all, my greatest thanks are given to our heavenly Father and our Lord Jesus Christ for the great revelation of this secret. Today, it is our Father's strong desire that all His sons discover what has become the lost secret of Christianity. He wants every member of the Body of Christ to be fully instructed and empowered with the knowledge of this Great Secret. He has told us in His Word that He appointed it for our glory and for the obedience of faith in the Church.

Epilogue

Every Christian who believes and walks in the truths of the Great Secret receives great blessings from God into their lives.

In reading this book, I believe that God has worked in your heart so that you too may comprehend the breadth and length and depth and height of the Great Secret concerning Christ and the Church. Therefore, I encourage you to walk and grow in the greatness of this revelation that was first given to the Apostle Paul.

God appointed the Great Secret for your glory. It is Christ who is in you and you are God's very best. You are His elect. You are a member of the One Body of Christ, the Temple of the Living God. I pray that you will continue in these truths and excel to the edifying of the Body of Christ which are God's will for your life.

Volume 2 of this book will be made available in time to come. There is a lot more to understand about the vastness of the revelation of the Great Secret. May God bless your life and strengthen you with might by His spirit in the inner man as you continue to enjoy the greatest secret of all time in the obedience of faith.

Further copies of this book and other information can be ordered from:

http://www.thegreatsecret.org

God bless you richly in the name of Jesus Christ,

Mark Atkinson

JHVH

****

282

Further Information

Further copies of this book and other resources on the Great Secret may be ordered from

http://www.thegreatsecret.org

This book is also available in large print version, hardback version and as an electronic download from the above website.

284